An Introduction to the Discount Factor Models

Towards Stocks

Alexander Hübbert

Published by Lulu Press, Inc.
www.lulu.com

ISBN: 978-1-716-40487-0 (paperback)

First paperback edition November 2020

Preface

Financial magazines and analysts issue recommendations on stocks considered attractive. These could be constructed on reasonable fundamentals (or technical) but cognitive biases could impede as "wishful thinking". Research have suggested that recommendations (by magazines and analysts) are inefficient compared to the theoretical models of quantifying the stock price[1]. Therefore, it is of paramount to understand how these models are structured as it brings clarity and logical modifications. The purpose of this book is to provide the reader with the essential concepts and steps for valuing stocks. Complexity has been avoided as much as possible since it could bring unanswered questions. Hence, the methodology of this book has been to provide the reader with simple structured derivations. Further, research will be presented to improve the comprehension.

Valuation needs to be adjusted conditionally on the circumstances and to what environment the company is operating in (not to mention the business model). This book will provide the fundamentals needed to further comprehend the modifications and assumptions required.

I would like to express my gratitude towards both Linus Johansson and Mattias Orava as their insights and guidance were of great help throughout the making of this book. Further the discussions and support from friends and colleagues have been greatly appreciated.

---

[1] Fried, D., D. Givoly (1982). Financial analysts' forecasts of earnings: a better surrogate for market expectations, Journal of Accounting and Economics, 4(2), pp. 85-107 and Brown L. D., Richardson G. D., Schwager S. J. (1987). An information interpretation of financial analyst superiority in forecasting earnings, Journal of Accounting Research, Spring, 25(1), pp. 49-67.

Contents

Chapter 1. Generic overview of the models

"Everything should be made as simple as possible, but not simpler"

-     *Albert Einstein*

"Truth is ever to be found in the simplicity, and not in the multiplicity and confusion of things."

-     *Isaac Newton*

To commence, the underlying elements of the models will be presented as to predefine before its modifications (contingent on the cash flow in Ch. 2). The distinction between the present and future value will be discussed, ending the chapter with the two-stage discount cash flow model in section 1.3.

1.0 Present and the Future Value

In generic, an investment (I) is expected to provide a return (r). The expected value of this investment could be written as:

$$I_0 + I_0 r = I_0(1 + r) = I_T$$

In some course literature, they would use E to denote the expected value of I_T as $E[I_0]$. But it would only complicate the structure of the coming models, not improving. Therefore, E will not be used but the reader should be aware that r is dynamic in practice and there are difficulties by estimate an accurate r. This subject will be discussed later in this chapter. I_0 is called the *present value* (PV) while I_T as the *future value* (FV):

$$PV(1 + r) = FV$$

Where r describes the percentage change from period 0 to i:

$$r_i = \frac{x_i - x_0}{x_0}$$

x_i can be replaced with FV and x_0 with PV:

$$r = \frac{FV - PV}{PV} \Rightarrow r = \frac{FV}{PV} - 1 \Rightarrow 1 + r = \frac{FV}{PV} \Rightarrow PV(1 + r) = FV$$

FV can be extended for an unknown period of times, which is the reason why the end time is denoted as i (being unspecified). Before proceeding with the definition of *PV* and *FV*, an example will be illustrated. If a stock is hold, the returns will be compounding, meaning that the capital gain (or loss) is reinvested (indirectly). For instance, assume an investment by 100 SEK in XYZ with a stock price of 100 SEK in the beginning of 2018. In the end of 2018, XYZ generated a return, adjusted for dividends and splits, of 10%. The investment grows to 110 SEK by the end of 2018.

$$I_0(1 + r_1) = I_1 \Rightarrow 100(1 + 0.1) = 110 \; SEK$$

It can further be assumed that the shareholder has an optimistic view of XYZ's performance for 2019, and by default chooses not to sell. But in the end of 2019, the stock price decreased by 20% by an unexpected change in XYZ's costumer behaviour. The investment in the end of 2019 became 88 SEK:

$$I_1(1 + r_2) = I_2 \Rightarrow 110[1 + (-0.2)] = 88 \; SEK$$

This can also be written as:

$$100(1 + 0.1)[1 + (-0.2)] = 88 \; SEK = I_0(1 + r_1)(1 + r_2) = I_2$$

If $r_1 = r_2$:

$$PV(1 + r_1)(1 + r_2) = PV(1 + r_1)^2 = FV$$

As the time frame could be unknown, for when the stock is sold, it would be preferable to replace 2 with n (or any other unspecified letter):

$$PV(1 + r_1)^n = FV$$

Where:

$$PV = \frac{FV}{(1 + r_1)^n}$$

This illustrates the definition of the *time value of money*. A rational investor prefers to receive a sum of money today rather than receiving the same sum of money in the future. The present value, as entitled, is today's value of the expected value in the future (*FV*). r has different synonyms conditioned on the circumstances. In this example, r is called the discount rate and $1/(1 + r_1)^n$ as the discount factor since an expected future value is being "discounted" back to its present.

In generic, r is constituted of variables as the risk-free interest rate and a premium that reflects the risk associated with a stock because of its uncertainty. The premium is normally called the *risk premium* which is the excess return of a stock (or more commonly an index) over the risk-free asset. There are distinctive models to quantify the discount rate which will be demonstrated in chapter 3.

To choose the correct discount rate when dealing with stocks (and decisions) are of importance. For instance, an investor could be faced with two different choices. One could be receiving a guarantee sum of money in the future (risk-free) and the other today. The choice depends on the size of these different sum and what the potential return could be. To quantify, assume the investor could either receive 100 SEK today or 120 SEK in one year. The stock, of interest, has an expected return of 10%. By investing the 100 SEK at a return of 10%, the investor is expected to receive:

$$PV(1 + r_1)^n = FV \Rightarrow 100(1 + 0.1)^1 = 110$$

Which is less than the 120 SEK. Hence, the investor should pick the alternative that includes the 120 SEK in one year. The discounting of the future value would have led to the same result:

$$PV(1 + r_1)^n = FV \Rightarrow PV = \frac{FV}{(1 + r_1)^n} = \frac{120}{1 + 0.1} = 109.09 \; SEK > the \; first \; offer$$

There was a mistake done in this example, which is common. When two alternatives are being compared it is important to think about the size of the return but also its *relevance*. As it was guaranteed the investor would had receive the 120 SEK in one year, the investing of 100 SEK should had been in a risk-free asset as the return of a risk-free asset is, per se, a guarantee. A stock's return is uncertain. Hence the actual return could had been 30% or 50%.

The size of r has a great impact on the compounding effect. The table below illustrates how $(1 + r_1)^n$ is affected by changes in n and r:

n	2%	4%	6%	8%	10%
1	1.02	1.04	1.06	1.08	1.10
2	1.04	1.08	1.12	1.17	1.21
3	1.06	1.12	1.19	1.26	1.33
4	1.08	1.17	1.26	1.36	1.46
5	1.10	1.22	1.34	1.47	1.61
6	1.13	1.27	1.42	1.59	1.77
7	1.15	1.32	1.50	1.71	1.95
8	1.17	1.37	1.59	1.85	2.14
9	1.20	1.42	1.69	2.00	2.36
10	1.22	1.48	1.79	2.16	2.59

Increased time has a positive effect on $(1 + r_1)^n$ conditioned on $r > 0$, and the same goes for the size of r. To use the table above, what is the future value by investing 100 SEK in a stock after 10 years with an expected return of 6%:

$$PV(1 + r_1)^n = FV \Rightarrow 100 * 1.79 = 179 \text{ SEK}$$

After 6 years:

$$PV(1 + r_1)^n = FV \Rightarrow 100 * 1.42 = 142 \text{ SEK}$$

Be cautious, in practice, it is not possible to trade a stock at a fraction. For instance, one could not trade an IMB share for 3/5 of a share.

So far, r has been assumed to be static which is not the case in practice as the circumstances are dynamic rather than static. But a dynamic r could make the equations disorderly if $(1 + r)$ were expressed by themselves. Therefore, it would be preferable to express the compounding as:

$$PV(1 + r_1)(1 + r_2) \dots (1 + r_n) = PV \prod_{i=1}^{n} (1 + r_i)$$

5 Annuity

For the sake of simplicity, let us continue to use $PV(1+r_1)^n = FV$ if not necessary.

1.1 Annuity

As a stock could pay out dividends (Div) to an investor, the future value could be expressed as:

$$PV(1+r_1)^n = FV \Rightarrow P_0(1+r_1) = P_1 + Div_1$$

Where P is the stock price.

By dividing the left-hand side (LHS) and right-hand side (RHS) with $(1+r_1)$, the P_0 is:

$$P_0 = \frac{P_1 + Div_1}{(1+r_1)}$$

This can be approached differently. The return of a stock, with dividends, is:

$$r_1 = \frac{P_1 - P_0 + Div_1}{P_0} = \frac{P_1 + Div_1}{P_0} - 1 \Rightarrow (1+r_1)P_0 = P_1 + Div_1 \Rightarrow P_0 = \frac{P_1 + Div_1}{(1+r_1)}$$

If the shareholder were interested in selling the stock after 2 years, the equation above would be extended with its dividends and discount factors as:

$$P_0 = \frac{Div_1}{(1+r_1)} + \frac{Div_2 + P_2}{(1+r_1)(1+r_2)}$$

As $P_0 = \frac{P_1 + Div_1}{(1+r_1)}$, it should also be true that $P_1 = \frac{P_2 + Div_2}{(1+r_2)}$, which can used to show that the equation above is correct:

$$r_2 = \frac{P_2 - P_1 + Div_2}{P_1} = \frac{P_2 + Div_2}{P_1} - 1 \Rightarrow (1+r_2)P_1 = P_2 + Div_2 \Rightarrow P_1 = \frac{P_2 + Div_2}{(1+r_2)}$$

Leading to:

$$P_0 = \frac{P_1 + Div_1}{(1+r_1)} = \frac{Div_1}{(1+r_1)} + \frac{P_1}{(1+r_1)} = \frac{Div_1}{(1+r_1)} + \frac{\frac{P_2 + Div_2}{(1+r_2)}}{(1+r_1)}$$

$$= \frac{Div_1}{(1+r_1)} + \frac{P_2 + Div_2}{(1+r_2)(1+r_1)}$$

What is the future value of this equation? With some algebra it can illustrated by first multiplying the LHS and RHS with $(1 + r_1)$:

$$P_0(1 + r_1) = \frac{Div_1}{(1 + r_1)}(1 + r_1) + \frac{Div_2 + P_2}{(1 + r_1)(1 + r_2)}(1 + r_1) = Div_1 + \frac{Div_2 + P_2}{(1 + r_2)}$$

The same for $(1 + r_2)$:

$$P_0(1 + r_1)(1 + r_2) = Div_1(1 + r_2) + \frac{Div_2 + P_2}{(1 + r_2)}(1 + r_2)$$

$$= Div_1(1 + r_2) + Div_2 + P_2 = FV$$

Notice $Div_1(1 + r_2)$, the shareholder would receive dividends in period 1 which is assumed to be reinvested at an expected return of r_2. These calculations could distinctly be expressed as:

$$P_0 = \sum_{t=1}^{n} \frac{Div_t}{(1 + r)^t} + \frac{P_n}{(1 + r)^n} = PV$$

$$P_0 \sum_{t=1}^{n}(1 + r)^t = \sum_{t=1}^{n} Div_t (1 + r)^{n-t} + P_n = FV$$

And if the returns differ:

$$P_0 = \frac{Div_1}{(1 + r_1)} + \frac{Div_2}{(1 + r_1)(1 + r_2)} + \cdots + \frac{Div_n}{(1 + r_1)(1 + r_2) * \ldots * (1 + r_n)} + \frac{P_n}{(1 + r)^n}$$

$$= PV$$

$$P_0 \prod_{t=1}^{n}(1 + r_t) = Div_1(1 + r_2) * \ldots * (1 + r_n) + Div_2(1 + r_3) * \ldots * (1 + r_n) + Div_n$$

$$+ P_n = FV$$

$\sum_{t=1}^{n} \frac{Div_t}{(1+r)^t} + \frac{P_n}{(1+r)^n}$ is called the present value of an *annuity*, which is the present value of a stream of cash flows paid at regular intervals. As an example, what is the stock price of Volvo if the shareholder expects to sell the stock at 120 SEK after 5 years where Volvo will pay 5 SEK per share in dividends? The discount rate is assumed to remain constant at 11%:

7 Annuity

$$P_0 = \sum_{t=1}^{5} \frac{Div_t}{(1+r)^t} + \frac{P_n}{(1+r)^n}$$

$$= \frac{5}{(1+0.11)} + \frac{5}{(1+0.11)^2} + \frac{5}{(1+0.11)^3} + \frac{5}{(1+0.11)^4} + \frac{5}{(1+0.11)^5}$$

$$+ \frac{120}{(1+0.11)^5} \approx 89.69\ SEK$$

If it was assumed that both the dividends and discount rates would be dynamic rather than static with the following dividends [4,7,3,9,2] and discount rates [7%, 8%, 10%, 11%, 5%]:

$$P_0 = \frac{4}{(1+0.07)} + \frac{7}{(1+0.0.7)(1+0.08)} + \frac{3}{(1+0.07)(1+0.08)(1+0.10)}$$

$$+ \frac{9}{(1+0.07)(1+0.08)(1+0.10)(1+0.11)}$$

$$+ \frac{2}{(1+0.07)(1+0.08)(1+0.10)(1+0.11)(1+0.05)}$$

$$+ \frac{120}{(1+0.07)(1+0.08)(1+0.10)(1+0.11)(1+0.05)}$$

$$\approx 100.88\ SEK$$

While it is necessary to break down the discounts as above, the equation could be simplified if the dividends and discounts were assumed to be static. The equation would then be:

$$P_0 = \sum_{t=1}^{n} \frac{Div_t}{(1+r)^t} + \frac{P_n}{(1+r)^n} = \frac{Div_1}{r}\left(1 - \frac{1}{(1+r)^n}\right) + \frac{P_n}{(1+r)^n}$$

A geometric progression can be used to prove this. The present value of dividends can be written as:

$$\sum_{t=1}^{n} \frac{Div_t}{(1+r)^t} = \frac{Div_1}{(1+r)^1} + \frac{Div_2}{(1+r)^2} + \frac{Div_3}{(1+r)^3} + \cdots + \frac{Div_n}{(1+r)^n}$$

Where Div remains static:

$$\frac{Div_1}{(1+r)^1} + \frac{Div_1}{(1+r)^2} + \frac{Div_1}{(1+r)^3} + \cdots + \frac{Div_1}{(1+r)^n}$$

$$= Div_1 \left[\frac{1}{(1+r)^1} + \frac{1}{(1+r)^2} + \frac{1}{(1+r)^3} + \cdots + \frac{1}{(1+r)^n} \right]$$

The $\left[\frac{1}{(1+r)^1} + \frac{1}{(1+r)^2} + \frac{1}{(1+r)^3} + \cdots + \frac{1}{(1+r)^n} \right]$ is called the *present value interest factor* of an annuity denoted as b and $\frac{1}{1+r}$ (discount factor) as a:

$$b = a + a^2 + a^3 + \cdots + a^n$$

And

$$ab = a^2 + a^3 + a^4 + \cdots + a^{n+1}$$

The LHS and RHS for b can be subtracted by ab:

$$b - ab = a - a^{n+1} \Rightarrow b(1-a) = a(1-a^n) \Rightarrow b = \frac{a(1-a^n)}{(1-a)}$$

Replace a with its denotation $\frac{1}{1+r}$ and multiply the RHS with $\frac{1+r}{1+r}$:

$$b = \frac{\frac{1}{1+r}\left(1 - \frac{1}{(1+r)^n}\right)}{\left(1 - \frac{1}{1+r}\right)} \frac{1+r}{1+r} = \frac{\frac{1+r}{1+r}\left(1 - \frac{1}{(1+r)^n}\right)}{\left(1 + r - \frac{1+r}{1+r}\right)} = \frac{\left(1 - \frac{1}{(1+r)^n}\right)}{(1 + r - 1)}$$

$$= \frac{\left(1 - \frac{1}{(1+r)^n}\right)}{r} = \frac{1}{r}\left(1 - \frac{1}{(1+r)^n}\right)$$

Since $\sum_{t=1}^{n} \frac{Div_t}{(1+r)^t} = Div_1 * b$, then:

$$\sum_{t=1}^{n} \frac{Div_t}{(1+r)^t} = Div_1 * b = \frac{Div_1}{r}\left(1 - \frac{1}{(1+r)^n}\right)$$

So:

$$P_0 = \sum_{t=1}^{n} \frac{Div_t}{(1+r)^t} + \frac{P_n}{(1+r)^n} = \frac{Div_1}{r}\left(1 - \frac{1}{(1+r)^n}\right) + \frac{P_n}{(1+r)^n}$$

$\frac{Div_1}{r}$ is referred to as the *terminal value*.

9 Annuity

Returning back to the example about Volvo with a constant dividend stream and discount rates, the equation above would yield the same stock price as $\sum_{t=1}^{n} \frac{Div_t}{(1+r)^t} + \frac{P_n}{(1+r)^n}$:

$$P_0 = \frac{Div_t}{r}\left(1 - \frac{1}{(1+r)^n}\right) + \frac{P_n}{(1+r)^n} = \frac{5}{0.11}\left(1 - \frac{1}{(1+0.11)^5}\right) + \frac{120}{(1+0.11)^5}$$

$$\approx 89.69 \; SEK$$

What if the shareholder does not expect to receive any dividends for the first 2 years? With $P_0 = \sum_{t=3}^{n=5} \frac{Div_t}{(1+r)^t} + \frac{P_n}{(1+r)^n}$ one would not make any mistake by pricing the stock:

$$P_0 = \frac{5}{(1+0.11)^3} + \frac{5}{(1+0.11)^4} + \frac{5}{(1+0.11)^5} + \frac{120}{(1+0.11)^5} \approx 81.13 \; SEK$$

However, if $\frac{Div_1}{r}\left(1 - \frac{1}{(1+r)^n}\right) + \frac{P_n}{(1+r)^n}$ was used without any consideration, one could mistakenly compute P_0 as:

$$P_0 = \frac{5}{0.11}\left(1 - \frac{1}{(1+0.11)^5}\right) + \frac{120}{(1+0.11)^5} \approx 89.69 \; SEK$$

As noticed, $\frac{Div_t}{r}\left(1 - \frac{1}{(1+r)^n}\right) + \frac{P_n}{(1+r)^n} \neq \sum_{t=1}^{n} \frac{Div_t}{(1+r)^t} + \frac{P_n}{(1+r)^n}$ conditioned on dividends being disturbed at $t > 1$. The term needed to be adjusted is $\frac{Div_t}{r}\left(1 - \frac{1}{(1+r)^n}\right)$. First, n for dividends should be equal to three (since it is three dividends being distributed) and multiplied with $\frac{1}{(1+r)^2}$ (discounting back to today):

$$P_0 = \frac{5}{0.11}\left(1 - \frac{1}{(1+0.11)^3}\right)\frac{1}{(1+0.11)^2} + \frac{120}{(1+0.11)^5} \approx 81.13 \; SEK$$

Being in accordance with $\sum_{t=1}^{n} \frac{Div_t}{(1+r)^t} + \frac{P_n}{(1+r)^n}$. This can be derived by using the geometric progression with an amendment:

$$\sum_{t=3}^{5} \frac{Div_t}{(1+r)^t} = Div\left[\frac{1}{(1+r)^3} + \frac{1}{(1+r)^4} + \frac{1}{(1+r)^5}\right]$$

$$= Div \left[\frac{1}{(1+r)^1} + \frac{1}{(1+r)^2} + \frac{1}{(1+r)^3}\right]\frac{1}{(1+r)^2}$$

As before $\left[\frac{1}{(1+r)^1} + \frac{1}{(1+r)^2} + \frac{1}{(1+r)^3}\right]$ denoted as b and $\frac{1}{(1+r)}$ as a:

$$b = a + a^2 + a^3$$

And

$$ab = a^2 + a^3 + a^4$$

The LHS and RHS for b is subtracted by ab:

$$b - ab = a - a^4 \Rightarrow b(1-a) = a(1-a^3) \Rightarrow b = \frac{a(1-a^3)}{(1-a)}$$

And replace a with $\frac{1}{(1+r)}$ and multiply the RHS with $\frac{1+r}{1+r}$

$$b = \frac{\frac{1}{1+r}\left(1 - \frac{1}{(1+r)^3}\right)}{\left(1 - \frac{1}{1+r}\right)}\frac{1+r}{1+r} = \frac{\left(1 - \frac{1}{(1+r)^3}\right)}{r} = \frac{1}{r}\left(1 - \frac{1}{(1+r)^3}\right)$$

Since $\sum_{t=3}^{n=5}\frac{Div_t}{(1+r)^t} = Div_3 * b \frac{1}{(1+r)^2}$:

$$Div_3 * b \frac{1}{(1+r)^2} = \frac{Div_3}{r}\left(1 - \frac{1}{(1+r)^3}\right)\frac{1}{(1+r)^2}$$

Therefore, if dividends were to be expected after t years, the simplified annuity model can be expressed as:

$$\sum_t^n \frac{Div_t}{(1+r)^t} + \frac{P_n}{(1+r)^n} = \frac{Div_t}{r}\left(1 - \frac{1}{(1+r)^{n-t}}\right)\frac{1}{(1+r)^t} + \frac{P_n}{(1+r)^n}$$

However, $\sum_t^n \frac{Div_t}{(1+r)^t} + \frac{P_n}{(1+r)^n}$ should be used in case of $r_1 \neq r_2$ and/or dividends being irregular distributed.

As for the future value $(PV[1+r]^n)$, where $PV = \frac{Div}{r}\left(1 - \frac{1}{(1+r)^n}\right) + \frac{P_n}{(1+r)^n}$:

11 Annuity

$$PV = \frac{Div_t}{r}\left(1 - \frac{1}{(1+r)^n}\right) + \frac{P_n}{(1+r)^n} \Rightarrow PV(1+r)^n = FV$$

$$= \frac{Div_t}{r}\left(1 - \frac{1}{(1+r)^n}\right)(1+r)^n + \frac{P_n}{(1+r)^n}(1+r)^n$$

$$= \frac{Div_t}{r}\left((1+r)^n - 1\right) + P_n = FV$$

While it would not tell whether one should invest in a stock (indirectly) it would suggest the expected wealth after n years provisory the Div_t remains static and the selling price is known.

So far, the present value of annuity with no growth has been dealt with. It is more common that $Div_1 \neq Div_2$, $P_0 \neq P_n$ and $r_1 \neq r_2$. The first and second problem could be amended by using a growth term g:

$$P_0 = \sum_{t=1}^{n} \frac{Div_{t-1}(1+g)^t}{(1+r)^t} + \frac{P_n}{(1+r)^n} = \sum_{t=1}^{n} \frac{Div_{t-1}(1+g)^t}{(1+r)^t} + \frac{P_0\left(1+g_p\right)^n}{(1+r)^n}$$

Note $Div_{t-1}(1+g)^t$, at the start ($t = 0$), $Div_{t-1}(1+g)^t = Div_0(1+g) = Div_1$. Further, it is assumed that the price is expected to grow differently compared to the dividends, g_p (geometric mean growth). This formula can be modified, for instance, with $\prod_{p=1}^{n}(1+g_p)$ if the movements of the stock price are known. In practice, it is of great difficulty to estimate an accurate future price. Fortunate, this can be adjusted with the help of perpetuity model, which will soon be presented. The $\sum_{t=1}^{n} \frac{Div_{t-1}(1+g)^t}{(1+r)^t} + \frac{P_n}{(1+r)^n}$, conditioned on the discount rates and growth remaining static, could be simplified as:

$$P_0 = \sum_{t=1}^{n} \frac{Div_{t-1}(1+g)^t}{(1+r)^t} + \frac{P_0(1+g)^n}{(1+r)^n} = \frac{Div_1}{r-g}\left(1 - \frac{(1+g)^n}{(1+r)^n}\right) + \frac{P_n}{(1+r)^n}$$

For the derivation, a geometric progression is used again:

$$\frac{Div_0(1+g)^1}{(1+r)^1} + \frac{Div_0(1+g)^2}{(1+r)^2} + \frac{Div_0(1+g)^3}{(1+r)^3} + \cdots + \frac{Div_0(1+g)^n}{(1+r)^n}$$

$$= Div_0\left[\frac{(1+g)^1}{(1+r)^1} + \frac{(1+g)^2}{(1+r)^2} + \frac{(1+g)^3}{(1+r)^3} + \cdots + \frac{(1+g)^n}{(1+r)^n}\right]$$

Where $\left[\frac{(1+g)^1}{(1+r)^1} + \frac{(1+g)^2}{(1+r)^2} + \frac{(1+g)^3}{(1+r)^3} + \cdots + \frac{(1+g)^n}{(1+r)^n}\right]$ denoted as b and $\frac{(1+g)}{(1+r)}$ as a:

$$b = a + a^2 + a^3 + \cdots + a^n$$

And

$$ab = a^2 + a^3 + a^4 + \cdots + a^{n+1}$$

The LHS and RHS for b is subtracted by ab:

$$b - ab = a - a^{n+1} \Rightarrow b(1 - a) = a(1 - a^n) \Rightarrow b = \frac{a(1 - a^n)}{(1 - a)}$$

Replace a with $\frac{(1+g)}{(1+r)}$ and multiply the RHS with $\frac{1+r}{1+r}$:

$$b = \frac{\frac{(1+g)}{(1+r)}\left(1 - \frac{(1+g)^n}{(1+r)^n}\right)}{\left(1 - \frac{(1+g)}{(1+r)}\right)} \frac{1+r}{1+r} = \frac{(1+g)\left(1 - \frac{(1+g)^n}{(1+r)^n}\right)}{(1+r-1-g)}$$

$$= \frac{(1+g)\left(1 - \frac{(1+g)^n}{(1+r)^n}\right)}{(r-g)} = \frac{(1+g)}{r-g}\left(1 - \frac{(1+g)^n}{(1+r)^n}\right)$$

And at last:

$$\sum_{t=1}^{n} \frac{Div_0(1+g)^n}{(1+r)^t} = Div_0 * b = \frac{Div_1}{r-g}\left(1 - \frac{(1+g)^n}{(1+r)^n}\right)$$

Conditioned on $r > g \geq 0$. Hence:

$$P_0 = Div_0 * b + \frac{P_0(1+g)^n}{(1+r)^n} = \frac{Div_1}{r-g}\left(1 - \frac{(1+g)^n}{(1+r)^n}\right) + \frac{P_n}{(1+r)^n}$$

If dividends were expected to be distributed after year t (same derivation as without growth):

$$P_0 = \sum_{t}^{n} \frac{Div_{t-1}(1+g)^t}{(1+r)^t} + \frac{P_0(1+g)^n}{(1+r)^n}$$

$$= \frac{Div_t}{r-g}\left(1 - \frac{(1+g)^{n-t}}{(1+r)^{n-t}}\right)\frac{1}{(1+r)^t} + \frac{P_n}{(1+r)^n}$$

Concluding, the structure of annuity changes, as the assumptions and/or modifications changes. Therefore, it is important to understand how the derivation were made so it can be modified after one's self assumptions and/or modifications.

It should be clarified that assuming no growth in dividends with static discount rates expressed as:

$$P_0 = \frac{Div_1}{r}\left(1 - \frac{1}{(1+r)^n}\right) + \frac{P_n}{(1+r)^n}$$

Implicit imply either that the dividends in year 1 (Div_1) is equal to the dividends in year 0 or the dividends after year 1 are not growing. The denotation of 1 is just a matter of specifying the time period rather than growth. Therefore, be careful when reading other analysis whether Div_1 is a product of the dividends in year 0 and a growth rate.

1.2 Perpetuity

The perpetuity model facilitates the approximation of the theoretical price as it is not needed to estimate what the stock price would be at the expected sell day. A *perpetuity* is a security that never ends paying a stream of cash flows. This would be expressed as:

$$P_0 = \frac{Div_1}{r}$$

If dividends were the cash flows of interest. Going back to an annuity with no growth:

$$P_0 = \frac{Div_1}{r}\left(1 - \frac{1}{(1+r)^n}\right) + \frac{P_n}{(1+r)^n}$$

Perpetuity means per definition "forever". The discount factor, with an infinity number of periods, can be expressed as:

$$\lim_{n \to \infty} \frac{1}{(1+r)^n}$$

As n moves to infinity, the discount factor becomes 0. In the table below, it is assumed $r = 10\%$, as n increases the discount factor moves closer to 0:

n	$\dfrac{1}{(1+r)^n}$
1	0.91
2	0.83
3	0.75
4	0.68
5	0.62
6	0.56
7	0.51
8	0.47
10	0.39
11	0.35
12	0.32
13	0.29
14	0.26
15	0.24
16	0.22

Hence:

$$\lim_{n \to \infty} \frac{1}{(1+r)^n} = 0$$

Conditioned on $r > 0$. The *perpetuity model* is retrieved by substituting this in the annuity:

$$\frac{Div_t}{r}\left(1 - \lim_{n \to \infty} \frac{1}{(1+r)^n}\right) = \frac{Div_t}{r}(1 - 0) = \frac{Div_t}{r}$$

The same holds for $\frac{Div_0(1+g)}{r-g}\left(1 - \frac{(1+g)^n}{(1+r)^n}\right)$:

$$\lim_{n \to \infty} \frac{(1+g)^n}{(1+r)^n} = 0$$

Provisory on $r > g \geq 0$. Hence:

$$\frac{Div_0(1+g)}{r-g}\left(1 - \lim_{n\to\infty}\frac{(1+g)^n}{(1+r)^n}\right) = \frac{Div_0(1+g)}{r-g}(1-0) = \frac{Div_0(1+g)}{r-g}$$

The $\frac{Div_0(1+g)}{r-g}$ is normally referred to as a *growing perpetuity model* or the *Gordon Growth Model*. Moving forward, $Div_0(1+g) = Div_1$, as the conclusion of perpetuity would not change regardless if $\frac{Div_1}{r-g}\left(1 - \frac{(1+g)^{n-1}}{(1+r)^n}\right)$ or $\frac{Div_0(1+g)}{r-g}\left(1 - \frac{(1+g)^n}{(1+r)^n}\right)$ is used.

As the assumption states that the cash flows are a never ending, the expected price to sell the stock would disappear. Implementing $\lim_{n\to\infty}\frac{1}{(1+r)^n}$ and $\lim_{n\to\infty}\frac{(1+g)^n}{(1+r)^n}$ for both non-growing and growing annuity models:

$$P_0 = \frac{Div_1}{r}\left(1 - \frac{1}{(1+r)^n}\right) + \frac{P_n}{(1+r)^n}$$

$$= \frac{Div_1}{r}\left(1 - \lim_{n\to\infty}\frac{1}{(1+r)^n}\right) + P_0 * \lim_{n\to\infty}\frac{1}{(1+r)^n}$$

$$= \frac{Div_0}{r}(1-0) + P_0 * 0 = \frac{Div_0}{r}$$

And:

$$P_0 = \frac{Div_1}{r-g}\left(1 - \frac{(1+g)^n}{(1+r)^n}\right) + \frac{P_n}{(1+r)^n}$$

$$= \frac{Div_1}{r-g}\left(1 - \lim_{n\to\infty}\frac{(1+g)^n}{(1+r)^n}\right) + P_0 * \lim_{n\to\infty}\frac{(1+g_p)^n}{(1+r)^n}$$

$$= \frac{Div_1}{r-g}(1-0) + P_0 * 0 = \frac{Div_1}{r-g}$$

As for Volvo, if the dividends are expected to remain at 4 SEK per share, with a growth of 2% and discount rate at 8%, the stock price should be:

$$P_0 = \frac{Div_0(1+g)}{r-g} = \frac{4(1+0.02)}{0.08 - 0.02} = 68\ SEK$$

1.3 Two-Stage Discount Cash Flow Model

So far, it is known that $P_0 = \frac{Div_1}{(r-g)}$ from the derivations used to quantify the stock price under the assumption that the business will continue to operate forever (and pay out cash flows). But some firms grow with different speed over time. This is altered by using the same assumptions as before:

$$P_0 = \frac{Div_1}{r-g}\left(1 - \frac{(1+g)^n}{(1+r)^n}\right) + \frac{P_n}{(1+r)^n} = \frac{Div_1}{r-g}\left(1 - \frac{(1+g)^n}{(1+r)^n}\right) + \frac{\frac{Div_{n+1}}{r_{n+1} - g_{n+1}}}{(1+r)^n}$$

Note that if $P_0 = \frac{Div_1}{(r-g)}$ then $P_n = \frac{Div_{n+1}}{(r_{n+1}-g_{n+1})}$. To be plain, P_n can be written as:

$$P_n = \frac{Div_{n+1}}{r_{n+1} - g_{n+1}}\left(1 - \frac{(1+g_{n+1})^T}{(1+r_{n+1})^T}\right) + \frac{P_T}{(1+r)^T}$$

As $\lim\limits_{T\to\infty} \frac{(1+g)^T}{(1+r)^T} = 0$:

$$P_n = \frac{Div_{n+1}}{r_{n+1} - g_{n+1}}\left(1 - \frac{(1+g_{n+1})^T}{(1+r_{n+1})^T}\right) + \frac{P_T}{(1+r)^T} = \frac{Div_{n+1}}{r_{n+1} - g_{n+1}}(1 - 0) + P_T * 0$$

$$= \frac{Div_{n+1}}{r_{n+1} - g_{n+1}}$$

Conditioned on $r > g \geq 0$. This equation is called *two-stage discount cash flow model* since the expected growth (or proportions) in cash flows is separated into two different time periods

Assume the shareholder expects Volvo to distribute dividends of 14 SEK per share that exceeds the status quo for 3 years and thereafter dividends of 7 SEK per share will be received. As Volvo pays a higher dividend for the first 3 years, we adjust the discount rate so it reflects the increase in the expected return and decrease after the 3 years, $r_{1-3} = 9\%$ and $r_{4-\infty} = 5\%$:

$$P_0 = \frac{Div_1}{r}\left(1 - \frac{1}{(1+r)^n}\right) + \frac{\frac{Div_{n+1}}{r_{n+1}}}{(1+r)^n} = \frac{14}{0.09}\left(1 - \frac{1}{(1+0.09)^3}\right) + \frac{\frac{7}{0.05}}{(1+0.09)^3}$$

$$\approx 143.54\ SEK$$

The equation can be elaborate into a three-stage model by introducing t as the time left between the growing perpetuity models and n:

$$\frac{Div_1}{r_n - g_n}\left(1 - \frac{(1 + g_n)^n}{(1 + r_n)^n}\right) + \frac{Div_{n+1}}{r_{n+1} - g_{n+1}}\left(1 - \frac{(1 + g_t)^t}{(1 + r_t)^t}\right)\frac{1}{(1 + r_t)^n}$$

$$+ \frac{\dfrac{Div_{t+n+1}}{(r_{t+n+1} - g_{t+n+1})}}{(1 + r_t)^{t+n}} = P_0$$

Equal to:

$$P_0 = \sum_{i=1}^{n}\frac{Div_{i-1}(1 + g)^i}{(1 + r)^i} + \sum_{v=n+1}^{t}\frac{Div_{v-1}(1 + g)^v}{(1 + r)^v} + \frac{Div_{t+n+1}}{(r_{t+n+1} - g_{t+n+1})}\frac{1}{(1 + r)^{t+n}}$$

Both the two-stage and three stage are customed towards stocks that are in their early stage of expansion, for example small caps. However, they can be used for larger stocks if it is expected that there will be some deviations, as for the example with Volvo. While Volvo remains as a large cap stock on the OMXS30 as today (2020), there could be abnormalities where Volvo decides to pay out a large proportion of its cash and cash equivalents to its shareholders. Based on empirical analysis, it is common to use a two-stage model where the forecasts are for the first 3-5 years.

Whether one should use dividends as the main component in these models or some other cash flows will be discussed in the coming chapter. Therefore, one should see these models using an undetermined cashflow (CF) and not a specific:

$$\sum_{i=1}^{n}\frac{Div_{i-1}(1 + g)^i}{(1 + r)^i} \Rightarrow \sum_{i=1}^{n}\frac{CF_{i-1}(1 + g)^i}{(1 + r)^i}$$

$$\frac{Div_t}{r - g}\left(1 - \frac{(1 + g)^n}{(1 + r)^n}\right) \Rightarrow \frac{CF_t}{r - g}\left(1 - \frac{(1 + g)^n}{(1 + r)^n}\right)$$

$$\frac{Div_t}{(r - g)} \Rightarrow \frac{CF_t}{(r - g)}$$

1.4 Summary

To summarize, whether a static fundamental model should be used is conditional on the assumptions by the user. What the objective is further amplifies the choice between the static and dynamic model. As seen, it is essential to discount back the perpetuity component or else a theoretical overestimation will occur. If a stock is believed to have a cash flow that differs in its estimated volatility, a two-stage discount cash flow model would be preferable as it helps to differentiate these distinctive periods.

Questions for chapter 1

1. With an expected return of 5% the first three years and 8% the last two years, what is the expected sell price if today's price is 80 SEK for stock A?

2. With a static discount rate of 10%, what should the theorical price be for stock B if stock B distributed a dividend per share of 6 SEK at year 5 and the expected stock price to sell at year 6 is 130 SEK?

3. It is expected that stock C will distribute dividends of 6 SEK in year 1, expected to remain constant with a growth of 1%. What should the theorical price of stock C with discount rates of [7%, 6%, 9%, 8%, 10%], expecting selling the stock for 240 SEK at year 5?

4. If the discount rates were expected to remain constant at 7% in question 3, what should the theorical price be? Further, what would the difference between prices (question 3 & 4) be if the selling price were unknown?

5. Stock D expects to start distributing dividends of 11.5 SEK per share after year 5. What should the theorical price of stock D if selling price was unknown?

6. With following information:

	Year 1-5	Year 6-∞
Growth	7%	2%
Dividends	4 SEK at year 1	
Discount rates	14%	6%

What is the theorical stock price for stock E?

7. With following information:

	Year 1-5	Year 6-7	Year 8-∞
Growth	5%	4.5%	2%
Dividends	10 SEK at year 1		
Discount rates	13%	11%	7%

What is the theorical stock price for stock F?

1.5 Appendix

Till now the r_i has been described as:

$$1 + r_i = \frac{x_i}{x_0} \Rightarrow 1 + r_i = \frac{P_i}{P_0}$$

Which is called *simple annually return*, describing a linear relationship between the return and the price of a stock. But what if *ln* was involved on the RHS before 1 is subtracted on both sides:

$$r_i = \frac{P_i}{P_0} - 1 \Rightarrow ln\,(r_i) = ln\left(\frac{P_i}{P_0} - 1\right) = ln\left(\frac{P_i}{P_0}\right)$$

As *ln* of $1 = 0$. If the return was described as $ln\left(\frac{P_i}{P_0}\right)$ then one is dealing with *continuous compounding return*:

$$e^{r_i} = \frac{P_i}{P_0} \Rightarrow ln\left(\frac{P_i}{P_0}\right) = ln(e^{r_i}) = r_i$$

Where this relationship should be familiar since:

$$e^{r_i} = \frac{P_i}{P_0} \Rightarrow P_0 = \frac{P_i}{e^{r_i}} = e^{-r_i}P_i$$

The continuous compounding return implies that the return on a security is reinvested back at an infinity numbers of period. Meaning:

$$\lim_{i \to \infty}\left(1 + \frac{r}{i}\right)^i \approx 2.718281828459 \approx e^r$$

However, if investments were reinvested every day (365) than the relationship above would be approximately true to if the investments were reinvested every second. Hence:

$$\lim_{i \to 365}\left(1 + \frac{r}{365}\right)^{365} \approx \lim_{i \to \infty}\left(1 + \frac{r}{i}\right)^i = e^r$$

Be aware that there is 252 trading days per year so using 365 could be partly, to a certain extent, deceptive.

21 Appendix

Why bother with continuous compounding? The issue with simple return is that it is not time-additive. For instance, assume that $P_0 = 40$, $P_1 = 50$ and $P_2 = 60$, then:

$$r_1 = \frac{50}{40} - 1 = 0.25$$

And

$$r_2 = \frac{60}{50} - 1 = 0.2$$

It should follow $r_1 + r_2 = \frac{P_2}{P_0} - 1$:

$$\frac{P_2}{P_0} - 1 = \frac{60}{40} - 1 = 0.5 \neq 0.25 + 0.2$$

That is because the return of a stock cannot be described by a linear relationship. But it can be amended with the natural logarithm:

$$r_1 + r_2 = \ln\left(\frac{50}{40}\right) + \ln\left(\frac{60}{50}\right) = \ln\left(\frac{60}{40}\right) = \ln(1 + 0.25) + \ln(1 + 0.2) = \ln(1 + 0.5)$$

Continuous compounding return is preferable compared to the simple return for several reasons. The main reason is the assumption about normal distribution for log transformed returns as it follows the Geometric Brownian motion. The importance of a normal distribution will later be described. Further, the log of prices is time-additive. One could argue that in real time, a stock's return gets compounded every day (minutes if so) supporting the hypothesis of using continuous compounding returns. The difference between the log and simple return would not differ significantly if the range between two prices are small, but as the spread increases, so does the deviation.

If one were asked to compute the return or discount a certain cash flow, it should be asked whether the return should be annually, monthly, weekly, or daily compounded. It can be preferable to make it daily because of the properties mentioned. But it also depends as it is not practical to discount dividends with continuous compounding discounts since it is not expected to receive a fraction of dividends each day. The structure will remain the same with some small changes. Just replace $(1+r)^t$ with $(1+r/i)^{it}$ and for the continuously compounded return, replace $(1+r)^t$ with e^{rt}. For instance, if the dividends were monthly compounded where the discounts and dividends remain static:

$$\sum_{t=1}^{12n} \frac{Div_t}{(1+r)^t} = \frac{Div_1}{\left(1+\frac{r}{12}\right)} + \frac{Div_1}{\left(1+\frac{r}{12}\right)^2} + \frac{Div_1}{\left(1+\frac{r}{12}\right)^3} + \cdots + \frac{Div_1}{\left(1+\frac{r}{12}\right)^{12n}}$$

$$= Div_1 \left[\frac{1}{\left(1+\frac{r}{12}\right)} + \frac{1}{\left(1+\frac{r}{12}\right)^2} + \frac{1}{\left(1+\frac{r}{12}\right)^3} + \cdots + \frac{1}{\left(1+\frac{r}{12}\right)^{12n}}\right]$$

Denote $\left[\frac{1}{\left(1+\frac{r}{12}\right)} + \frac{1}{\left(1+\frac{r}{12}\right)^2} + \frac{1}{\left(1+\frac{r}{12}\right)^3} + \cdots + \frac{1}{\left(1+\frac{r}{12}\right)^{12n}}\right]$ as b and $\frac{1}{\left(1+\frac{r}{12}\right)}$ as a:

$$b = a + a^2 + a^3 + \cdots + a^n$$

And

$$ab = a^2 + a^3 + a^4 + \cdots + a^{n+1}$$

Subtract the LHS and RHS for b with ab:

$$b - ab = a - a^{n+1} \Rightarrow b(1-a) = a(1-a^n) \Rightarrow b = \frac{a(1-a^n)}{(1-a)}$$

Replace a with $\frac{1}{\left(1+\frac{r}{12}\right)}$ and multiply the RHS with $\frac{\left(1+\frac{r}{12}\right)}{\left(1+\frac{r}{12}\right)}$:

$$b = \frac{\frac{1}{\left(1+\frac{r}{12}\right)}\left(1 - \frac{1}{\left(1+\frac{r}{12}\right)^{12n}}\right)}{\left(1 - \frac{1}{\left(1+\frac{r}{12}\right)}\right)} \frac{\left(1+\frac{r}{12}\right)}{\left(1+\frac{r}{12}\right)} = \frac{\frac{\left(1+\frac{r}{12}\right)}{\left(1+\frac{r}{12}\right)}\left(1 - \frac{1}{\left(1+\frac{r}{12}\right)^{12n}}\right)}{\left(\left(1+\frac{r}{12}\right) - \frac{\left(1+\frac{r}{12}\right)}{\left(1+\frac{r}{12}\right)}\right)}$$

23 Appendix

$$= \frac{\left(1 - \frac{1}{\left(1+\frac{r}{12}\right)^{12n}}\right)}{\left(1+\frac{r}{12}-1\right)} = \frac{\left(1 - \frac{1}{\left(1+\frac{r}{12}\right)^{12n}}\right)}{\frac{r}{12}} = \frac{1}{\frac{r}{12}}\left(1 - \frac{1}{\left(1+\frac{r}{12}\right)^{12n}}\right)$$

$$= \frac{12}{r}\left(1 - \frac{1}{\left(1+\frac{r}{12}\right)^{12n}}\right)$$

And since $\frac{Div}{\left(1+\frac{r}{12}\right)^1} + \frac{Div}{\left(1+\frac{r}{12}\right)^2} + \frac{Div}{\left(1+\frac{r}{12}\right)^3} + \cdots + \frac{Div}{\left(1+\frac{r}{12}\right)^{12n}} = Div_1 * b$:

$$\frac{Div_1}{\left(1+\frac{r}{12}\right)^1} + \frac{Div_1}{\left(1+\frac{r}{12}\right)^2} + \frac{Div_1}{\left(1+\frac{r}{12}\right)^3} + \cdots + \frac{Div_1}{\left(1+\frac{r}{12}\right)^{12n}} = Div_1 * b$$

$$= \frac{Div_1}{\frac{r}{12}}\left(1 - \frac{1}{\left(1+\frac{r}{12}\right)^{12n}}\right)$$

Hence:

$$P_0 = \frac{Div_1}{\frac{r}{12}}\left(1 - \frac{1}{\left(1+\frac{r}{12}\right)^{12n}}\right) + \frac{P_n}{\left(1+\frac{r}{12}\right)^{12n}}$$

To emphasize, Div_1 in this context is a twelfth fraction of an annually dividend.

The structure of the annuity model with continuous compounded returns/discounts will be like previous:

$$\sum_{t=1}^{n} \frac{Div_t}{e^{rt}} = \frac{Div_1}{e^{r1}} + \frac{Div_2}{e^{r2}} + \frac{Div_3}{e^{r3}} + \cdots + \frac{Div_n}{e^{rn}}$$

Where Div remains static:

$$\frac{Div_1}{e^{r1}} + \frac{Div_2}{e^{r2}} + \frac{Div_3}{e^{r3}} + \cdots + \frac{Div_n}{e^{rn}} = Div_1\left[\frac{1}{e^{r1}} + \frac{1}{e^{r2}} + \frac{1}{e^{r3}} + \cdots + \frac{1}{e^{rn}}\right]$$

The $\left[\frac{1}{e^{r1}} + \frac{1}{e^{r2}} + \frac{1}{e^{r3}} + \cdots + \frac{1}{e^{rn}}\right]$ as present value interest factor of an annuity denoted as b and $\frac{1}{e^r}$ as a:

$$b = a + a^2 + a^3 + \cdots + a^n$$

And

$$ab = a^2 + a^3 + a^4 + \cdots + a^{n+1}$$

The LHS and RHS for b can be subtracted by ab:

$$b - ab = a - a^{n+1} \Rightarrow b(1 - a) = a(1 - a^n) \Rightarrow b = \frac{a(1 - a^n)}{(1 - a)}$$

Replace a with its denotation $\frac{1}{1+r}$ and multiply the RHS with $\frac{1+r}{1+r}$:

$$b = \frac{\frac{1}{e^r}\left(1 - \frac{1}{e^{rn}}\right)e^{r1}}{\left(1 - \frac{1}{e^r}\right)e^{r1}} = \frac{\frac{e^r}{e^r}\left(1 - \frac{1}{e^{rn}}\right)}{\left(e^r - \frac{e^r}{e^r}\right)} = \frac{\left(1 - \frac{1}{e^{rn}}\right)}{(e^r - 1)} = \frac{1}{e^r - 1}\left(1 - \frac{1}{e^{rn}}\right)$$

Since $\sum_{t=1}^{n}\frac{Div_t}{e^{rt}} = Div_1 * b$, then:

$$\sum_{t=1}^{n}\frac{Div_t}{e^{rt}} = Div_1 * b = \frac{Div_1}{e^r - 1}\left(1 - \frac{1}{e^{rn}}\right)$$

As for growth, following the generic derivation will lead to

$$\sum_{t=1}^{n}\frac{Div_{t-1}e^{gt}}{e^{rt}} = Div_0 * b = \frac{Div_0 e^g}{e^r - e^g}\left(1 - \frac{e^{gn}}{e^{rn}}\right)$$

And if the dividends were expected to be distributed after v years

$$\sum_{t=v}^{n}\frac{Div_t}{e^{rt}} = \frac{Div_1}{e^r - 1}\left(1 - \frac{1}{e^{rn}}\right)\frac{1}{e^{r(t-1)}}$$

Chapter 2. Cash flows

"If you look at academic studies, you can see that stock prices are most closely correlated with cash flow. It's such a straightforward number. Cash flow is what will drive shareholder returns."

-     Jeff Bezos

"If I had to run a company on three measures, those measures would be customer satisfaction, employee satisfaction and cash flow."

-     Jack Welch

This chapter presents the cash flows used in the models described in chapter 1. To avoid misconception, empirical analysis will be presented. There are conflicting results in research despite that all these models, adjusted for the chosen cash flows, have the equivalent theoretical fundamentals. Therefore, it is essential to see why these adjusted models differ (section 2.7). Since chapter 1 used dividends as a cash flow (plus the expected stock price), the section about dividends will be short but critical as the derivation of the other cash flows uses the relationship with the dividends.

2.0 Dividends

In its essence, dividends are a distribution of wealth, from the company to the shareholders. From chapter 1:

$$P_0 = \frac{P_1 + Div_1}{(1 + r_1)}$$

This model is called the *Discount Dividend Model* (DDM), which can be modified in different ways conditioned on the assumptions. There are two essential parts of DDM which can be displayed by decomposing r_1:

$$P_0 = \frac{P_1 + Div_1}{(1 + r_1)} \Rightarrow P_0(1 + r_1) = P_1 + Div_1 \Rightarrow 1 + r_1 = \frac{P_1}{P_0} + \frac{Div_1}{P_0} \Rightarrow r_1$$

$$= \frac{P_1 - P_0}{P_0} + \frac{Div_1}{P_0}$$

$\frac{P_1-P_0}{P_0}$ is called the *capital gain* rate while $\frac{Div_1}{P_0}$ is called *dividend yield*, and the sum of these is the *total return*. This could reveal whether a company is dividend orientated. If not, dividends should not be the cash flow used.

Frequently, companies pay out dividends if these have earned a positive net income (NI). One can see, in annual reports, that dividend policy is, in generic, specified as a percentage of net income, called the *dividend pay-out ratio* (DPR). Therefore, dividends could be written as a function of the earnings and dividend pay-out ratio:

$$Div_1 = \frac{TNI_1}{outstanding\ shares} * DPR = NI_1 * DPR$$

Where NI_1 is the net income per share at year 1 and TNI_1 as total net income year 1. Dividends may increase for reasons such as:

1. NI increases.
2. Outstanding shares decreases.
3. DPR increases.

This new function of Div_1 can be used in DDM:

$$P_0 = \frac{P_1 + NI_1 * DPR}{(1 + r_1)}$$

Recall that Div_1 could be assumed to be equivalent to $Div_0(1 + g)$ where g can be defined as the retention rate (more information on section 2.1) multiplied with return on equity (ROE). Hence:

$$P_0 = \frac{P_1 + (NI_0 * DPR)(RR_1 * ROE_1)}{(1 + r_1)}$$

There are disputes whether investors prefer the capital gain, or the dividend yield contingent on taxes. Companies need to pay additional taxes if they distribute dividends, since dividends, per se, are not deductible despite paying taxes on the earnings before taxes, hence the expression "double taxation". Having international stocks and not domestic could create further tax disadvantages. As for Sweden, *investment savings accounts* (ISK), replaces the 30% taxation on the dividends (domestic stocks) and capital gains for the investor with a standard taxation on the whole value of the shareholder's account at each quarter. This taxation is the government borrowing rate + one percentage unit with a total lower limit of 1.25 % in Sweden. This only applies to domestic stock and not foreign.

Some would argue, despite the tax disadvantage, that dividends are a materialised wealth where free cash flow to equity is not which reduces the risk of losing money. For instance, a company could choose not to pay any dividends, leading to a high reinvestment rate and free cash flow for the coming years, mirrored in the stock price. However, the firm could have a bad year, as for Swedbank and Danske bank under the money laundering scandal at the end of 2018 and beginning of 2019, which caused a great drop in their respective stock price. After it calmed down, the capital gain could have been eliminated or even negative (depended on when it was bought).

The tax disadvantage could be measured, not accurate but it would give a good picture. Assume that the stock price before the ex-dividend day is denoted as P_B and at the day as P_A, where the tax on capital is denoted as t_{cap} and on dividends as t_{Div}. The price paid for the stock is denoted as P. The return if the stock were sold before the ex-dividend day (the day not being authorized for dividends) would be:

$$r_B = P_B - (P_B - P)t_{cap}$$

While the return at the ex-dividend day given that the stock is sold:

$$r_A = P_A - (P_A - P)t_{cap} + Div(1 - t_{Div})$$

If the investors were indifferent between selling before or at ex-dividend day, then $r_B = r_A$ needs to hold:

$$P_B - (P_B - P)t_{cap} = P_A - (P_A - P)t_{cap} + Div(1 - t_{Div}) \Rightarrow \frac{P_B - P_A}{Div} = \frac{(1 - t_{cap})}{(1 - t_{Div})}$$

Which tells the price drop on the-dividend day has to reflect the tax differential between the capital tax and dividend tax. Another way to put this would be to compare $P_B - P_A$ with Div:

$$P_B - Div \ = P_A \Rightarrow Indifferent\ between\ dividends\ and\ capital\ gains$$

$$P_B - Div < P_A \ \Rightarrow Dividends\ are\ more\ heavily\ taxed$$

$$P_B - Div > P_A \ \Rightarrow Capital\ gains\ are\ more\ heavily\ taxed$$

There has been a great debate whether dividends are a hedge for inflation or not. In order to obtain an asset that functions as a hedge for inflation, the nominal return must be equal or greater than the rate of inflation. As far back as 1970, Reilly, Johnson & Smith[2] results indicated that a group of common stocks were not consistent or complete inflation hedge, which means that the statement that common stocks could be used as an inflation hedge cannot be accepted. Between 1968 and 1980, common stocks lost a lot of values in real terms. Moore (1980)[3] claims that tax factors had a huge role, especially for dividends as dividends are exposed to double taxation. But mainly, dividend behaviour has contributed to this mismatch. However, Farrell (1985)[4] argues that dividends, in the long run, works as a hedge against inflation. But Farrell agree with Moore that during 1965-74, dividends did not provide a hedge against inflation as dividends were lagged behind the rate of inflation. So, over shorter intervals, the hedge might be unbalance while in the long-run dividends have proved to offer a good hedge against inflation. With the growing perpetuity dividend model, an unanticipated increase in inflation (I) can be factored:

$$P = \frac{Div_1(1 + I)}{r_e(1 + I) - g(1 + I)}$$

[2] Reilly, F., Johnson, G., & Smith, R. (1970). Inflation, Inflation Hedges, and Common Stocks. Financial Analysts Journal, 26(1), 104-110. Retrieved June 1, 2020, from www.jstor.org/stable/4470632

[3] MOORE, B. (1980). The Curious Case of Common Stocks. Challenge, 23(4), 20-27. Retrieved June 1, 2020, from www.jstor.org/stable/40719894

[4] Farrell, J. (1985). The Dividend Discount Model: A Primer. Financial Analysts Journal, 41(6), 16-25. Retrieved June 1, 2020, from www.jstor.org/stable/4478881

If an increase (or decrease) in inflation, reflects an equal proportion in each component, then:

$$P = \frac{Div_1(1 + I)}{(r_e - g)(1 + I)} = \frac{Div_1}{(r_e - g)}$$

Therefore, mismatches could be because of different increase in the proportions.

2.1 Free Cash Flow

The main difference between free cash flow and dividends is that dividends are actual limited payments to shareholders (or stakeholders) where free cash flows is the total theoretical amount that could be paid out. Hence, the models used for a *Discounted Cash Flow Model* (DCF) do not differ from DDM. There are two different type of free cash flows, one that accounts for all the stakeholders (FCFF) and the other for the shareholders (FCFE). FCFF stands for "*Free Cash Flow to the Firm*" which are the cash flows that are available to all the stakeholders after capital expenditure ($CAPEX$) has been accounted, while FCFE stands for "*Free Cash Flow to equity*" which are the cash flows available for the shareholders after CAPEX, net change of debts and interest expenses have been accounted. It will be easy to see the distinction between the two by looking at how these two cash flows are calculated:

$$FCFF = EBIT(1 - t_c) + dep\ \&\ amor - CAPEX - \Delta NWC$$

$$FCFE = Net\ income + dep\ \&\ amor - CAPEX - \Delta NWC - (Debt\ paid$$
$$- Debt\ issued)$$

EBIT is earnings before interest and taxes. FCFF adjust for EBIT after taxes (t_c) while FCFE does not because interest expenses are an income for the debt holders (being a part of the stakeholders). Another distinction is $-(Debt\ paid - Debt\ issued)$, which follows the same reasoning. The other components are *dep* (depreciation), *amor* (amortization, which is deprecation on intangible assets) and ΔNWC (change in net non-cash working capital).

The CAPEX is defined as the change in gross property plant and equipment. One could also replace the gross with net if its available. But if the change in net gross property plant and equipment would be used, then the deprecation in the calculation of FCF should not be added as the net change already contain the deprecation (as subtracted), resulting in a double count. Therefore, one should be aware of how CAPEX is defined as further adjustments could be needed.

The equations above could be unsuitable as the calculations are simple compared to that of reality. The free cash flows need to be further adjusted for other non-cash items. Fortunately, the cash flow from operating activities (CFOA), in reports, considers the sources and uses of cash from its daily activities which also regards the non-cash (income & expenses) items. So, the equations could be rewritten as:

$$FCFF = CFOA + interest\ expenses\ (1 - tc) - CAPEX$$

$$FCFE = CFOA - CAPEX - (Debt\ paid - Debt\ issued)$$

But CFOA uses the net income instead of EBIT after taxes, which is why FCFF is needed to be adjusted by adding back the interest expenses after tax. It should be mentioned that in some cases both FCFF and FCFE need to be amended for any gain of asset sale after taxes. For instance, a company could sell one of its equipment as it has no use any longer. Then the gain (or loss) would be the market value of the equipment subtracted by its book value, where the book value is the purchase price (at initiation) subtracted with the accumulated depreciation. So:

$$FCFF = CFOA + interest\ expenses\ (1 - tc) - CAPEX \\ + (Sales\ price - gain\ on\ sale * t_c)$$

$$FCFE = CFOA - CAPEX - (Debt\ paid - Debt\ issued) \\ + (Sales\ price - gain\ on\ sale * t_c)$$

The opportunity cost of not selling the equipment while its market value is above the book value, should be subtracted from the cash flows. Because of its complexity, one could assume that the sales price is expected, on average, to be in line with its book value.

All cash flows are needed to be "per share" because different size of cash flows does not say much until they are comparative with the stock price. Let us say that stock A and B have the following values from 2015-18:

Stock A in MSEK	2015	2016	2017	2018
CFOA	325	300	350	400
CAPEX	20	40	60	80
Debt paid	50	40	30	60
Debt issued	20	30	80	40
FCFE	275	250	340	300
Outstanding shares	10	10	12	12
FCFE per share	27.50	25	28.33	25
Stock B in MSEK	2015	2016	2017	2018
CFOA	500	600	650	625
CAPEX	50	60	70	80
Debt paid	90	80	75	60
Debt issued	40	40	30	20
FCFE	400	500	535	505
Outstanding shares	20	20	20.5	20.5
FCFE per share	20	25	26.10	24.63

While stock B has a greater $FCFE$, it is lesser per share, meaning that shareholders in stock B are entitled to a less proportion of FCFE than of those in stock A. But two objects are missing, what is the stock price today and what should it be based on the cash flows? Assume that the stock price for A is 200 SEK and for B it is 250 SEK. Further, the discount rate for A is 8.5% and 10% for B (implying that B carries a greater risk) where both stocks expect to grow their FCFE with 2%. By the usage of the perpetuity model $\left(\frac{CF(1+g)}{r-g} \Rightarrow \frac{FCFE(1+g)}{r-g}\right)$, the stock price for A and B should be:

$$P_A = \frac{25(1 + 0.02)}{0.085 - 0.02} = 392.31 > 200$$

And

$$P_B = \frac{24.63(1 + 0.02)}{0.1 - 0.02} = 318.75 > 250$$

As the stock price for both A and B are less than their theoretical, it indicates a buy signal. In reality, one has to further analyse the companies' previous performance as it could be that FCFE for stock A is deviating from it past because of an anomaly, which does not expect to remain. Then a two-stage model might be more appropriate. Also, one can be constrained by its budget so it is not always the case that all signals should be followed. Further, as these models are exposed to subjective assumptions, it is of high probability that different investor will get different theoretical prices despite being exposed to same information.

Personally, I would recommend using financial websites as Morningstar as they make it easier to compute cash flows as FCFF, FCFE and other cash flows that we will continue to discuss. However, be caution of their definitions. For instance, Morningstar defines the free cash flow (FCF) as *"Free cash flow represents the cash a company has left over after investing in the growth of its business"* hence, $FCF = CFOA - CAPEX$. So, if one uses Morningstar, the FCFE or FCFF should be adjusted by $FCFE = FCF - (Debt\ paid - Debt\ issued)$ and $FCFF = FCF + interest\ expenses(1 - tc)$.

There are more modifications that could be accomplished when calculating FCFF and FCFE. The growth in EBIT (g_{ebit}) could be calculated as the product of the return on capital (ROC, sometimes replaced by $WACC$ "Weighted Average Cost of Capital") and the reinvestment rate (RR_{ebit}), which tells how much of the EBIT after taxes gets reinvested:

$$RR_{ebit} * ROC = g_{ebit}$$

RR_{ebit} is equal to the net capital expenditures ($CAPEX - dep$) plus the investments in non-cash working capital (ΔNWC) divided with $EBIT(1 - t_c)$:

$$RR_{ebit} = \frac{g_{ebit}}{ROC} = \frac{CAPEX - dep + \Delta NWC}{EBIT(1 - t_c)} = 1 - \frac{FCFF}{EBIT(1 - t_c)}$$

By using the above equation, FCFF can be simplified to:

$$RR_{ebit} = 1 - \frac{FCFF}{EBIT(1 - t_c)} \Rightarrow \frac{FCFF}{EBIT(1 - t_c)} = 1 - RR_{ebit}$$

$$\Rightarrow FCFF = (1 - RR_{ebit}) * EBIT(1 - t_c)$$

The same can be done for FCFE. As with RR_{ebit}, the retention rate (RR_n) considers the amount of net income that gets reinvested after the dividends have been paid out. By replacing ROC with ROE (return on equity, sometimes replaced by the required return of equity (r_e)):

$$RR_n * ROE = g_n$$

Where:

$$RR_n = \frac{g_n}{ROE} = \frac{CAPEX - dep + \Delta NWC}{Net\ income}$$

Therefore:

$$RR_n = \frac{CAPEX - dep + \Delta NWC}{Net\ income} \Rightarrow RR_n * Net\ income = CAPEX - dep + \Delta NWC$$

It can be seen by the equation above, on RHS, it misses net income, the net change of debts ($debt\ paid - debt\ issued$) and further $CAPEX - dep + \Delta NWC$ should be $-(CAPEX - dep + \Delta NWC)$ in order to get the FCFE. By amending for these and replacing $CAPEX - dep + \Delta NWC$ with $RR_n * Net\ income$:

$$FCFE = Net\ income - RR_n * Net\ income - (Debt\ paid - Debt\ issued)$$

$$\Rightarrow FCFE = Net\ income(1 - RR_n) - (Debt\ paid - Debt\ issued)$$

Moving forward, knowing what the growth in a model should be is of paramount. As mentioned, it could be defined as:

$$RR_n * ROE = g_n$$

This is a common assumption regarding when the dividends constitute as the cash flows. As, in annual reports, dividend payments are normally paid as a percentage of the net income, knowing how much of the net income that is reinvested (RR_n) and how much the return of the earnings was in relation to the equity (ROE) allows one to get a good picture of the growth in dividends. Therefore, RR_n could be specified as:

$$RR_n = \frac{NI_t - Div_t}{NI_t}$$

Further, growth conditioned on the expected inflation and GDP growth could as well be used. But growth in the stable conditioned (terminal value) should not exceed the expected growth in the GDP as that would indirectly assume the company to outgrow the country it operates in.

2.2 Enterprise Value

So far, it has been shown how to use FCFE and DDM to estimate the stock price, but FCFF could as well be used for the same purpose. First, the value of the firm, *Enterprise value* (EV), needs to be estimated. EV is calculated as:

$$EV = Market\ value\ of\ equity + Market\ value\ of\ debts - Cash$$

Where, in this example, a perpetuity model can be used (conditioned on the assumptions):

$$EV = \frac{FCFF_0(1 + g)}{WACC - g}$$

Assume the EBIT at the end of the year was 50 MSEK with a tax rate of 40%, depreciation of 4 MSEK, capital expenditure of 10 MSEK and a net change of non-cash working capital of 15 MSEK, a WACC of 10% and that these components in FCFF increase with the same proportion of 3% over the years (g). So, FCFF is:

$$FCFF_0 = 50(1 - 0.4) + 4 - 10 - 15 = 9$$

Hence:

$$EV = \frac{9 * 1.03}{0.1 - 0.3} \approx 132.5 \text{ MSEK}$$

By using RR, the example can be recreated by assuming (or calculate, $\frac{10-4+15}{50(1-0.4)}$) the firm invests a proportion of 70% of its EBIT after tax:

$$FCFF_0 = 50(1 - 0.4) * (1 - 0.7) = 9$$

Hence:

$$EV = \frac{9 * 1.03}{0.1 - 0.3} \approx 132.5 \; MSEK$$

The beauty of equations is how they can be decomposed:

$$EV = Market \; value \; of \; equity + Debts - Cash$$

Where:

$$Market \; value \; of \; equity = P_0 * outstanding \; shares$$

Assume the firm holds a total cash of 20 MSEK and debts of 50 MSEK with outstanding shares of 50 million, then the stock price should be:

$$EV = \frac{9 * 1.03}{0.1 - 0.3} \Rightarrow \frac{9 * 1.03}{0.1 - 0.3} = P_0 * 50 + 50 - 20 \Rightarrow P_0 = \frac{\left(\frac{9 * 1.03}{0.1 - 0.3} + 20 - 50\right)}{50}$$

$$\approx 2.05 \; SEK$$

It is common to use the book value of debts instead of its market value because of its complications to calculate the present value of all the debts the business possesses. One solution could be to assume that the market has the correct expectation of the business and could therefore value it correctly. Then the EV could be used, for instance, on Yahoo Finance by decomposing the equation to find out the market value of debts and later use it to make its own modifications/calculations:

$$EV - Market \; value \; of \; equity + Cash = Market \; value \; of \; debts$$

It should be mentioned that the context of debts involves interested bearing liabilities, while total liabilities are both debts and non-debts (non-interest bearing). In Sweden, there are no formal distinction between them two which could be puzzled at first. The EV could be extended by:

$EV =$	$+ Market\ value\ of\ equity$
	$+ Market\ value\ of\ debts$
	$+ Minority\ interest\ at\ market\ value$
	$+ Preferred\ equity\ at\ market\ value$
	$- Cash$

The EV is defined as the market value of the firm. One could also see EV as the sum of claims by creditors and shareholders or the theoretical takeover price if a company were to be bought. Per definition, a buyer of a company needs to pay, not only the price per share of each stock, but also the debt representatives at their market value. Also, minority interest shareholders, owning less than 50% of outstanding shares, would need to sell their shares. Further, those owning preferred equity, such as preferred stock that is a hybrid between a stock and a bond, would also be needed to be paid for their priority claim over the company. But as a buyer acquires a company, the buyer could use the company's cash and cash equivalents to pay off the debts. For the sake of simplicity, the definition of EV as *market value of equity + market value of debts − cash* will be used.

2.3 Residual Income Method

Per definition, the name, *Residual Income Method* (RIM), implies what is left over after the interest for the shareholders (their required return) has been taken care of. This method involves using the net income, equity and the discount rate (for shareholders). While from a stakeholder's perspective (Economic Value Added "EVA"), the EBIT after tax, capital employed (CE) and WACC are being used. Capital employed is the capital investments necessary for a business to function and it is calculated through taking the total assets subtracted with the current liabilities. Some would amend this by subtracting the non-interest-bearing debts from total assets instead of the current liabilities. But often, the current liabilities are the same as non-interest-bearing debts.

The residual method is commonly used when it is hard to calculate a firm's free cash flow or the dividends are low in relation to the stock price, e.g. insurance companies, real estate, investment companies and banks.

For shareholders, the market value of equity (ME) is its book value of equity (BE) for year t plus the present value of the residual incomes (RI) which are the net incomes (NI) adjusted for the required return by the shareholders:

$$RI_t = NI_t - r_e * BE_{t-1}$$

Leading to a market value of equity:

$$ME_0 = BE_0 + \sum_{t=1}^{T} \frac{RI_t}{(1+r_e)^t} = BE_0 + \sum_{t=1}^{T} \frac{NI_t - r_e * BE_{t-1}}{(1+r_e)^t}$$

Where the equation can be decomposed to calculate the stock price (P):

$$P_0 * S_0 = BE_0 + \sum_{t=1}^{T} \frac{RI_t}{(1+r_e)^t} \Rightarrow P_0 = \frac{BE_0 + \sum_{t=1}^{T} \frac{RI_t}{(1+r_e)^t}}{S_0}$$

But how can $P_0 * S_0 = BE_0 + \sum_{t=1}^{T} \frac{RI_t}{(1+r_e)^t}$ be mathematically correct? Well, let us return to the one-year dividend model in chapter 1 where:

$$P_0 = \frac{P_1 + D}{1 + r_e}$$

The book value of equity for time t can be described as:

$$BE_t = NI_t + BE_{t-1} - D$$

Given that there is no new issue of shares and repurchase of shares and clean surplus relation holds (CSI). For the sake of simplicity, it is assumed that this equation is expressed as per share. Now, rearrange the relationship as:

$$D = NI_t + BE_{t-1} - BE_t$$

Which can be inserted in the equation:

$$P_0 = \frac{P_1 + D}{1 + r_e} = \frac{P_1 + NI_1 + BE_0 - BE_1}{1 + r_e}$$

Add and subtract with $\frac{1+r_e}{1+r_e} BE_0$ on the RHS:

$$P_0 = \frac{P_1 + NI_1 + BE_0 - BE_1}{1 + r_e} - \frac{1 + r_e}{1 + r_e} BE_0 + \frac{1 + r_e}{1 + r_e} BE_0$$

$$= \frac{P_1 + NI_t + BE_0 - BE_1}{1 + r_e} - \frac{BE_0 + r_e BE_0}{1 + r_e} + BE_0$$

$$= \frac{P_1 + NI_t + r_e BE_0 - BE_1}{1 + r_e} + BE_0 = BE_0 + \frac{NI_t - r_e BE_0}{1 + r_e} + \frac{P_1 - BE_1}{1 + r_e}$$

Recall that $P_1 = \frac{P_2 + D}{1 + r_e}$, where solving for P_0 would lead to:

$$P_0 = \frac{D}{1 + r_e} + \frac{P_2 + D}{(1 + r_e)^2}$$

Using this relationship and both add and subtract with $\left(\frac{1+r_e}{1+r_e}\right)^2 BE_1$ [5]:

$$P_0 = BE_0 + \frac{NI_t - r_e BE_0}{1 + r_e} + \frac{P_1 - BE_1}{1 + r_e}$$

$$= BE_0 + \frac{NI_t - r_e BE_0}{1 + r_e} + \frac{P_2 + NI_2 + BE_1 - BE_2}{(1 + r_e)^2} - \frac{BE_1}{1 + r_e}$$

$$+ \frac{(1 + r_e)^2}{(1 + r_e)^2} BE_1 - \frac{(1 + r_e)^2}{(1 + r_e)^2} BE_1$$

$$= BE_0 + \frac{NI_1 - r_e BE_0}{1 + r_e} + \frac{NI_2 - r_e BE_1}{(1 + r_e)^2} + \frac{P_2 - BE_2}{(1 + r_e)^2}$$

As the number of years are extended, the relationship could be defined as:

---

[5] $\frac{(1+r_e)^2}{(1+r_e)^2} BE_1 = \frac{(1+r_e)BE_1 + (1+r_e)BE_1 r_e}{(1+r_e)^2} = \frac{(1+r_e)BE_1 + BE_1 r_e + BE_1 r_e^2}{(1+r_e)^2} = \frac{(1+r_e)BE_1}{(1+r_e)^2} + \frac{BE_1 r_e + BE_1 r_e^2}{(1+r_e)^2} =$

$\frac{BE_1}{1+r_e} + \frac{BE_1 r_e + BE_1 r_e^2}{(1+r_e)^2}$ and $-\frac{(1+r_e)^2}{(1+r_e)^2} BE_1 = -\frac{(1+r_e)BE_1 + (1+r_e)BE_1 r_e}{(1+r_e)^2} = -\frac{BE_1 + BE_1 r_e + BE_1 r_e + BE_1 r_e^2}{(1+r_e)^2}$

$$P_0 = BE_0 + \sum_{t=1}^{\infty} \frac{NI_t - r_e * BE_{t-1}}{(1+r_e)^t} + \frac{P_\infty - BE_\infty}{(1+r_e)^\infty}$$

What if the variables are expected to grow constant after year 0? Recall from chapter 1:

$$\sum_{t=1}^{n} \frac{Div_t}{(1+r)^t} = \frac{Div_1}{r}\left(1 - \frac{1}{(1+r)^n}\right)$$

Hence

$$\sum_{t=1}^{\infty} \frac{RI_{t-1}(1+g)^t}{(1+r_e)^t} = \frac{RI_0(1+g)}{r_e - g}\left(1 - \frac{(1+g)^\infty}{(1+r_e)^\infty}\right)$$

As:

$$RI_1 = NI_1 - r_e * BE_0 = (NI_0 - r_e BE_{-1})(1+g)$$

Conditioned on the variables remaining static. And second:

$$\lim_{t \to \infty} \left(\frac{1+g}{1+r_e}\right)^t = 0$$

Given $r_e > g$. Hence the stock price should be:

$$P_0 = BE_0 + \frac{RI_0(1+g)}{r_e - g}\left(1 - \frac{(1+g)^\infty}{(1+r_e)^\infty}\right) + \frac{P_\infty - BE_\infty}{(1+r_e)^\infty} = P_0 = BE_0 + \frac{NI_1 - r_e * BE_0}{r_e - g}$$

$P_\infty - BE_\infty$ are already imbedded with the growth ($P_\infty - BE_\infty = (P_0 - BE_0)(1 + g)^\infty$). But what if there is no growth associated with the company? It is known that:

$$P_0 = BE_0 + \sum_{t=1}^{\infty} \frac{NI_t - r_e * BE_{t-1}}{(1+r_e)^t} + \frac{P_\infty - BE_\infty}{(1+r_e)^\infty}$$

Where the previous annuity equation could be used:

$$P_0 = BE_0 + \sum_{t=1}^{\infty} \frac{NI_t - r_e * BE_{t-1}}{(1+r_e)^t} = BE_0 + \frac{RI_1}{r_e}\left(1 - \frac{1}{(1+r_e)^\infty}\right) + \frac{P_\infty - BE_\infty}{(1+r_e)^\infty}$$

Since $\frac{1}{(1+r_e)^\infty} = 0$ (chapter 1):

$$P_0 = BE_0 + \frac{RI_1}{r_e}\left(1 - \frac{1}{(1+r_e)^\infty}\right) + \frac{P_\infty - BE_\infty}{(1+r_e)^\infty} = BE_0 + \frac{RI_1}{r_e}$$

Recall $RI_1 = NI_1 - r_e BE_0$:

$$P_0 = BE_0 + \frac{NI_1 - r_e * BE_0}{r_e} = BE_0 + \frac{NI_1}{r_e} - \frac{r_e * BE_0}{r_e} = BE_0 + \frac{NI_1}{r_e} - BE_0 = \frac{NI_1}{r_e}$$

This non growing perpetuity model is called "Uthålliga Vinsten" in Swedish, translating to "Sustainable Profit".

One should be causation of how other use the RIM as some would define the relationship as:

$$P_0 = BE_0 + \sum_{t=1}^{\infty} \frac{(ROE - r_e)BE_{t-1}}{(1+r_e)^t} + \frac{P_\infty - BE_\infty}{(1+r_e)^\infty}$$

Where ROE is defined, according to them, as $\frac{NI_t}{BE_{t-1}}$. In my opinion, this could led to misinterpretation as ROE, in practice, is defined as $\frac{NI_t}{BE_t}$. If one were to use the $ROE = \frac{NI_t}{BE_t}$, then RIM would be wrongly calculated as that is not a part of the derivation.

Let us return to stock A and B example. Consider an investor at the end of year 2019 (Year 0) with the annual report for the whole year and the following projections of the companies between 2020-22:

Stock A in MSEK	2019 (0)	2020 (1)	2021 (2)	2022 (3)
NI	425	600	525	550
BE	5500	6100	6625	7175
r_e	0.08	0.08	0.08	0.05
Stock B in MSEK	2019 (0)	2020 (1)	2021 (2)	2022 (3)
NI	900	950	1000	1250
BE	8500	9450	10 450	11 400
r_e	0.09	0.09	0.09	0.065

Notice that BE increases with the size of NI. This is a logical argument since the company had reinvested all its earnings and not repurchased any shares. Certainly, this would not always be the case with projections.

Assume the following for the outstanding shares:

In M	2015	2016	2017	2018
Outstanding shares$_A$	10	10	10	10
Outstanding shares$_B$	20	20	20	20

It is assumed that the size of shares will remain unchanged as issues of new shares or repurchases would change the dynamic of the book value of equity. The last section will describe the effect of repurchases and new emission.

Per Share for A	2019 (0)	2020 (1)	2021 (2)	2022 (3)
RI_t^A		16.00	3.70	21.88
$\sum_{t=0}^{T} \dfrac{RI_t^A}{(1+r_e)^t}$		14.81	3.17	
$\dfrac{RI_{T+1}^A}{r_e}$ $\dfrac{}{(1+r_e)^T}$				375.09
BE_0^A	550.00			
P_0^A	943.07			
Per Share for B	2019 (0)	2020 (1)	2021 (2)	2022 (3)
RI_t^B		9.25	7.48	28.54
$\sum_{t=0}^{T} \dfrac{RI_t^B}{(1+r_e)^t}$		8.49	6.29	
$\dfrac{RI_{T+1}^B}{r_e}$ $\dfrac{}{(1+r_e)^T}$				369.53
BE_0^B	425.00			
P_0^B	809.31			

The procedures are specified below for stock A and B:

$$P_A = BE_0^A + \sum_{t=1}^{2} \frac{RI_t^A}{(1+r_e)^t} + \frac{\dfrac{RI_{T+1}^A}{r_{eT+1}}}{(1+r_e)^T}$$

$$= 550 + \frac{16}{(1+0.08)^1} + \frac{3.7}{(1+0.08)^2} + \frac{\dfrac{21.88}{0.05}}{(1+0.08)^2} = 943.07$$

And:

$$P_B = BE_0^B + \sum_{t=1}^{2} \frac{RI_t^B}{(1+r_e)^t} + \frac{\dfrac{RI_{T+1}^B}{r_{eT+1}}}{(1+r_e)^T}$$

$$= 425 + \frac{9.25}{(1+0.09)^1} + \frac{7.48}{(1+0.09)^2} + \frac{\dfrac{28.54}{0.065}}{(1+0.09)^2} = 809.31$$

As it can be seen, the P_0 differs significantly for both firms when the residual income method is used rather than $FCFE$. It should not be the case as the FCFE can be used to derive the same relationship, as for EVA later on. This will later be discussed with regards to the empirical analysis. But for these examples, they deviate as detailed relationship is not accounted for. Notice that $\frac{535.5-525}{525} = 0.02$ and $\frac{1010-1000}{1000} = 0.01$ regarding the growth. This does not always need to be the case as one could assume a different growth rate than the foregoing. If so, the model would be adjusted by extending with one (or further) discount factor. If one wondered about $\frac{P_\infty - BE_\infty}{(1+r_e)^\infty}$ from the derivation, it just disappears. The entire model can be specified as:

$$P_0 = BE_0 + \sum_{t=1}^{\infty} \frac{NI_t - r_e * BE_{t-1}}{(1+r_e)^t} + \frac{P_\infty - BE_\infty}{(1+r_e)^\infty}$$

Where in this case:

$$P_0 = BE_0 + \sum_{t=1}^{2} \frac{NI_t - r_e * BE_{t-1}}{(1+r_e)^t} + \sum_{t=3}^{\infty} \frac{NI_t - r_e * BE_{t-1}}{(1+r_e)^t} + \frac{P_\infty - BE_\infty}{(1+r_e)^\infty}$$

Which can be rewritten as:

$$P_0 = BE_0 + \sum_{t=1}^{2} \frac{NI_t - r_e * BE_{t-1}}{(1 + r_e)^t} + \frac{RI_3}{r_e}\left(1 - \frac{1}{(1 + r_e)^\infty}\right)\frac{1}{(1 + r_e)^2} + \frac{P_\infty - BE_\infty}{(1 + r_e)^\infty}$$

Recall $\lim_{T \to \infty} \frac{1}{(1+r_e)^T} = 0$, so:

$$P_0 = BE_0 + \sum_{t=1}^{2} \frac{NI_t - r_e * BE_{t-1}}{(1 + r_e)^t} + \frac{RI_3}{r_e}\left(1 - \frac{1}{(1 + r_e)^\infty}\right)\frac{1}{(1 + r_e)^2} + \frac{P_\infty - BE_\infty}{(1 + r_e)^\infty}$$

$$= BE_0 + \sum_{t=1}^{2} \frac{NI_t - r_e * BE_{t-1}}{(1 + r_e)^t} + \frac{RI_3}{r_e}(1 - 0)\frac{1}{(1 + r_e)^2} + (P_\infty - BE_\infty) * 0$$

$$= BE_0 + \sum_{t=1}^{2} \frac{NI_t - r_e * BE_{t-1}}{(1 + r_e)^t} + \frac{RI_3}{r_e}\frac{1}{(1 + r_e)^2}$$

Despite its restrictiveness how the book equity in year 1 was quantified, RIM has achieved abnormal returns (excess return over the index market). Pinochi, Fais & Corsiglia (2019)[6] research suggested, through a two-stage model, significant alphas could be achieved. Although they outperformed the analysts' recommendations, they used the analysts' forecast. Fried & Givoly (1982)[7] and Brown, Richardson & Schwager (1987)[8] results supported the idea of using analysts' estimates as it has acted as a better proxy. However, Bradshaw, Drake, Myers & Myers (2012)[9] argues that this only holds for large, mature and stable firms with a short horizon.

---

[6]Pinochi, Marco and Fais, Fabio and Corsiglia, Marco, Residual Income Model and Abnormal Returns: A Comparison to Factor Styles and Sell-Side Analysts (June 25, 2019). Business Valuation OIV Journal Spring 2019. Available at SSRN: https://ssrn.com/abstract=3478213 or http://dx.doi.org/10.2139/ssrn.3478213

[7] Fried, D., D. Givoly (1982). Financial analysts' forecasts of earnings: a better surrogate for market expectations, Journal of Accounting and Economics, 4(2), pp. 85-107

[8] Brown L. D., Richardson G. D., Schwager S. J. (1987). An information interpretation of financial analyst superiority in forecasting earnings, Journal of Accounting Research, Spring, 25(1), pp. 49-67.

[9] Bradshaw M. T., Drake M., Myers J., Myers L. (2012). A Reexamination of Analysts' Superiority over Time-Series Forecasts, Review of Accounting Studies, 17(4), pp. 944-968.

One main advantage of the residual income model, stated by Pinochi, Fais & Corsiglia (2019), is that it implies a lower weight of the terminal value. While the model is normally used for financial firms, it can still be used for companies that do not distribute any dividends or have a volatile free cash flow.

2.4 Economic Value Added

The *Economic Value Added* (EVA) accounts for the whole value of the company which involves a similar procedure as with RIM (with some amendments):

$$Residual\ Value\ Added_t\ (RVA_t) = EBIT_t(1 - t_c) - WACC * CE_{t-1}$$

Where:

$$EV_0 = CE_0 + \sum_{t=1}^{T} \frac{RVA_t}{(1 + WACC)^t}$$

$$= CE_0 + \sum_{t=1}^{T} \frac{EBIT_t * (1 - t_c) - WACC * CE_{t-1}}{(1 + WACC)^t}$$

The book value of the enterprise value (BEV), equal to the capital invested (CE, book equity + net debt), at year 1 can be written as:

$$BEV_1 = CE_1 = CE_0 + EBIT_1(1 - t_c) - FCFF_1$$

So:

$$FCFF_1 = CE_0 + EBIT_1(1 - t_c) - CE_1$$

Replace FCFF with the relationship above in DCF:

$$\frac{FCFF_1}{(1 + r_{WACC})} \Rightarrow \frac{EBIT_1(1 - t_c) - CE_1 + CE_0}{(1 + r_{WACC})}$$

Add and subtract $\frac{1+r_{WACC}}{1+r_{WACC}} CE_0$:

$$\frac{EBIT_1(1 - t_c) - CE_1 + CE_0}{(1 + r_{WACC})} + \frac{1 + r_{WACC}}{1 + r_{WACC}} CE_0 - \frac{1 + r_{WACC}}{1 + r_{WACC}} CE_0$$

$$= \frac{EBIT_1(1 - t_c) - CE_1 + CE_0}{(1 + r_{WACC})} + \frac{1 + r_{WACC}}{1 + r_{WACC}} CE_0 - \frac{1 + r_{WACC}}{1 + r_{WACC}} CE_0$$

$$= CE_0 + \frac{EBIT_1(1 - t_c) - CE_0 r_{WACC}}{(1 + r_{WACC})} - \frac{CE_1}{1 + r_{WACC}}$$

This should ring a bell. What happens If we extend it to 2 years? Well:

$$\frac{FCFF_1}{(1 + r_{WACC})} + \frac{FCFF_2}{(1 + r_{WACC})^2}$$

$$\Rightarrow \frac{EBIT_1(1 - t_c) - CE_1 + CE_0}{(1 + r_{WACC})} + \frac{EBIT_2(1 - t_c) - CE_2 + CE_1}{(1 + r_{WACC})^2}$$

$$= CE_0 + \frac{EBIT_1(1 - t_c) - CE_0 r_{WACC}}{(1 + r_{WACC})} - \frac{CE_1}{1 + r_{WACC}} + \frac{EBIT_2(1 - t_c) - CE_2 + CE_1}{(1 + r_{WACC})^2}$$

To continue, add and subtract with $\left(\frac{1 + r_{WACC}}{1 + r_{WACC}}\right)^2 CE_1$ and do like how it was previously done.

Although the whole company is valued, the equation can still be decomposed to quantify the stock price:

$$EV_0 = P_0 * S_0 + Market\ value\ of\ debts - Cash$$

$$\Rightarrow P_0 * S_0 + Market\ value\ of\ debts - Cash = CE_0 + \sum_{t=1}^{T} \frac{RVA_t}{(1 + WACC)^t}$$

$$\Rightarrow P_0 = \frac{CE_0 + \sum_{t=1}^{T} \frac{RVA_t}{(1 + WACC)^t} + Cash - Market\ value\ of\ debts}{S_0}$$

As an example, assume the following values for stock C and stock D:

Stock C in MSEK	2019 (0)	2020 (1)	2021 (2)	2022 (3)
EBIT	700	900	950	1000
CE	8000	9000	9500	10 000
WACC	0.06	0.06	0.06	0.04
Cash	150			
Debts	250			
Stock D in MSEK	2019 (0)	2020 (1)	2021 (2)	2022 (3)
EBIT	900	1000	1250	1500
CE	10 500	12 000	13 000	13 250
WACC	0.08	0.08	0.08	0.045
Cash	300			
Debts	600			

Where the tax rate is homogenous for both stocks at a rate of 40%. C and D has the same outstanding shares as A and B:

In M	2015	2016	2017	2018
Outstanding shares$_C$	10	10	10	10
Outstanding shares$_D$	20	20	20	20

Now it is possible to calculate P_0:

P_0 for C	2019 (0)	2020 (1)	2021 (2)	2022 (3)
RVA_t^C		60.00	30.00	220.00
$\displaystyle\sum_{t=1}^{T} \frac{RVA_t^C}{(1+WACC)^t}$		56.60	26.70	
$\displaystyle\frac{\frac{RVA_{T+1}^C}{WACC_{T+1}}}{(1+WACC)^T}$			4 894.98	
CE^C	8000			
$Cash$	150			
$Debts$	250			
P_0^C	1 287.83			

P_0 for D	2019 (0)	2020 (1)	2021 (2)	2022 (3)
RVA_t^D		-240.00	-210.00	315.00
$\displaystyle\sum_{t=1}^{T} \frac{RVA_t^D}{(1+WACC)^t}$		-222.22	-180.04	
$\displaystyle\frac{\frac{RVA_{T+1}^D}{WACC_{T+1}}}{(1+WACC)^T}$			6 001.37	
CE^D	10 500			
$Cash$	300			
$Debts$	600			
P_0^D	789.96			

Plugging into the formulas:

$$P_C = \frac{\left[\left(CE_0^C + \sum_{t=1}^{2}\frac{RVA_t^C}{(1+WACC)^t} + \frac{\frac{RVA_{T+1}^C}{WACC_{T+1}}}{(1+WACC)^T}\right) - Debts + Cash\right]}{S_0}$$

$$= \frac{\left[\left(8000 + \frac{60}{(1+0.06)^1} + \frac{30}{(1+0.06)^2} + \frac{\frac{220}{0.04}}{(1+0.06)^2}\right) - 250 + 150\right]}{10} = 1287.83$$

Where RVA_t for the first year:

$$RVA_1 = 900(1 - 0.4) - 0.06 * 8000 = 60 \ MSEK$$

And

$$P_D = \frac{\left[\left(CE_0^D + \sum_{t=1}^{2}\frac{RVA_t^D}{(1+WACC)^t} + \frac{\frac{RVA_{T+1}^D}{WACC_{T+1}}}{(1+WACC)^T}\right) - Debts + Cash\right]}{S_0}$$

$$= \frac{\left[\left(10\ 500 + \frac{-240}{(1+0.08)^1} + \frac{-210}{(1+0.08)^2} + \frac{\frac{315}{0.045}}{(1+0.08)^2}\right) - 600 + 300\right]}{20}$$

$$= 789.96$$

Where RVA_t for the first year:

$$RVA_1 = 1000(1 - 0.4) - 0.08 * 10\ 500 = -240 \ MSEK$$

Recall that $\sum_{t=1}^{T}\frac{RVA_t}{(1+WACC)^t}$ and $\sum_{t=1}^{T}\frac{RI_t}{(1+r_e)^t}$ can be valued differently based on one's assumptions and expectations. For instance, if it was thought that the firm was consistent in their cash flows, the two-stage model could had been replaced by the growing perpetuity model $\frac{RVA_1}{WACC-g}$ and $\frac{RI_1}{r_e-g}$.

Stephen (1996)[10] was the first to apply EVA, although it was already mentioned by Alfred Marshall in 1890. Stephen evaluated EVA for a period between 1985 and 1993 with the companies in the 1993 Stern Stewart Performance 1000 resulting in a sample of 7546 company valuation. Some were removed as they were not public traded all the nine years. Stephen concluded that while the free cash flow had less than 1% predictive power over the variation in the market/capital among the 6551 cases,

---

[10] Stephen, O. (1996). EVA and market value. Journal of Applied Corporate Finance. 9. 116-126. 10.1111/j.1745-6622.1996.tb00109.x.

EVA had approximately 31% where NOPAT (EBIT after taxes) had 33%. This is higher than the 5% of using the current year earnings which was conducted by Easton, Harris, & Ohlsson (1992)[11]. Further, Stephen's results exhibit that EVA explained 55% of the five-year changes in the market value, where earnings only explained 24% and EVA explained 74% of the ten-year changes while earnings explained 64%. Such significant discrepancy between the free cash flow and EVA, despite the usage FCFF to derive the relationship, is fascinating. This can be due to IAS 1 prior to 2009, which will be discussed later.

2.5 Net Asset Value

Net Asset Value (NAV) method is similar to residual method but there is an interest solely on company's book value of equity, hence the shareholders are of interest. The idea behind this is to provide the shareholder with a minimum price to sell the stock for. Indirectly, this would help the buyer to understand whether the stock is undervalued. If the company choose to liquidate its assets and pay of its liabilities, the shareholder would be left with book value of equity per share. Therefore, the minimum price should be:

$$P_0 = BE_0$$

This could be derived from RIM with two assumptions, the discount rate is equal to the return on equity and $NI_1 = NI_0$:

$$P_0 = BE_0 + \frac{NI_1 - r_e * BE_0}{r_e} \Rightarrow BE_0 + \frac{NI_1 - ROE_0 * BE_0}{ROE_0} = \frac{NI_1}{ROE_0} = \frac{NI_1}{\frac{NI_0}{BE_0}} = NI_1 \frac{BE_0}{NI_0}$$

As it was assumed that $NI_1 = NI_0$:

$$P_0 = NI_1 \frac{BE_0}{NI_0} = BE_0$$

---

[11] Easton, P., Harris, T, & Ohlsson, J. (1992). "Aggregate Accounting Earnings Can Explain Most of Security Returns: The Case of Long Return Intervals." Journal of Accounting and Economics 15, no. 2-3: 119-42.

It is straightforward to use but some adjustment can be used to get a more accurate picture of the book value of equity:

$Adjusted\ BE_0\ before\ t_c =$	$+\ Share\ of\ capital$
	$+\ Reserve\ fund$
	$+\ Retained\ earnings$
	$+\ Untaxed\ reserves\ (A)$
	$+\ Fair\ value\ of\ fixed\ asset\ -$
	$book\ value\ (B)$
	$+Fair\ value\ of\ inventory\ (book\ value$
	$-\ accumulated\ depreciation)(C)$
$Adjusted\ BE_0\ after\ t_c =$	$+\ Adjusted\ BE_0\ before\ t_c$
	$-\ (A + B + C) * t_c$

Notice that NAV is valued according to its market value, hence the total assets and liabilities are valued at its market value. It is common to use measurements as "Value in use" or "Liquidation value". Value in use is defined as the NPV of a cash flows or other benefits that an asset generates while liquidation value is the value retrieved if the assets were sold.

As these methods requires knowledge of market values for a specific asset and liabilities, it is recommended to use the book value of equity with the recommended adjustments, as it would be time consuming and complex otherwise.

As NAV method decompose the residual method and concentrate on the book value, its method applies to the same group of businesses as with the residual method. But for listed real estate companies, European Public Real Estate Association (EPRA) announced, 2016, guidelines for calculating the NAV with the purpose to be in line with IFRS and the interest of the stakeholders. Hence the name "EPRA NAV" might appear in listed real estate companies' annual report. *EPRA NAV* includes the NAV with adjustment to the fair value of properties, other investment interests and excluding items that are not expected to crystallise in a long-term investment property business model. While its calculation can be difficult to calculate due to the information needed, real estate companies publish EPRA NAV and EPRA NNAV, which is the EPRA NAV adjusted for the fair value of financial instruments, debt and deferred taxes. These were further updated in 2019 due the growth of *Real Estate Investment Trust (REIT)* regimes in Europe. REIT is an investment trust with a special regulation taxation. Hence, EPRA updated the guidelines to *"level the playing field between Non-REITs and REITs and ensure the EPRA BPR remain aligned with the International Financial Reporting Standards (IFRS) developments, through the inclusion of new adjustments in how real estate companies conduct their financial reporting"*.

It could be preferable for further adjustment as excluding intangible assets from the total asset when NAV is calculated. According to IAS 38 an intangible asset is:

"an identifiable non-monetary asset without physical substance. An asset is a resource that is controlled by the entity as a result of past events (for example, purchase or self-creation) and from which future economic benefits (inflows of cash or other assets) are expected."

Downfalls like the 2008 financial crisis and Covid-19 in 2020 have reminded investors to comprehend the value of a business underlying tangible assets. Goodwill is classified as an intangible asset where it includes the value of reputation, brand, intellectual property etc. The increase in goodwill occur when a buyer (company of interest) acquires an existing business and paid more than the net market value. If the buyer paid for less than the net market value, it would decrease, resulting in a "Badwill". But how accurate is it to value a reputation, brand etc? It can be diffused and therefore preferable to exclude the intangible assets from the total asset when the NAV is calculated.

For information of the relevance by IAS 40 and IFRS 13, as they regulate the calculations of NAV, see the Appendix.

2.6 Buybacks

A company could do buybacks if they considered their stock to be undervalued. While its fundamentals would not change if it used cash and cash equivalents (treasury shares increases, decreasing equity), it would if it increased its total debts (D_{Total}) resulting in a change in r_{wacc} (and indirectly r_e), and used these for buybacks. However, there are exemptions when using existence cash and cash equivalents would increase shareholders' value. This will be discussed later. As known:

$$EV_0 = P_0 * S_0 + D_0 - C_0$$

$$\Rightarrow EV_0 + \Delta EV_0 = P_0 * S_0 + D_0 - C_0 + \Delta(P_0 * S_0 + D_0 - C_0)$$

$$= P_0 * (1 + \Delta) * S_0 * (1 + \Delta) + D_0 * (1 + \Delta) - C_0 * (1 + \Delta)$$

Where the variables can be denoted as:

$$P_0 * (1 + \Delta) = P_1, S_0 * (1 + \Delta) = S_1, D_0 * (1 + \Delta) = D_1, C_0 * (1 + \Delta) = C_1$$

For the sake of simplicity, assume that r_{wacc} is the only variable that changes and a perpetuity model is used:

$$\Delta EV_0 = \Delta\left(\frac{FCFE_1}{r_{wacc0}}\right) = \frac{FCFE_1}{r_{wacc1}} - \frac{FCFE_1}{r_{waco}} = FCFE_1\left(\frac{1}{r_{wacc1}} - \frac{1}{r_{wacc0}}\right)$$

$$\Rightarrow FCFE_1\left(\frac{r_{wacc0} - r_{wacc1}}{r_{wacc1} * r_{wacc0}}\right)$$

Since:

$$EV_0 = \frac{FCFE_1}{r_{wacc0}} \Rightarrow EV_0 * r_{wacc0} = FCFE_1$$

This can be further simplified as:

$$FCFE_1\left(\frac{r_{wacc0} - r_{wacc1}}{r_{wacc1} * r_{wacc0}}\right) = EV_0 * r_{wacc0}\left(\frac{r_{wacc0} - r_{wacc1}}{r_{wacc1} * r_{wacc0}}\right) = EV_0\left(\frac{r_{wacc0} - r_{wacc1}}{r_{wacc1}}\right)$$

Returning back to the previous equation:

$$EV_0 + \Delta EV_0 = P_1 * S_1 + D_1 - C_1 = EV_0 + EV_0 \left(\frac{r_{wacc_0} - r_{wacc_1}}{r_{wacc_1}} \right)$$

$$= P_1 * S_1 + D_1 - C_1$$

Where the new price (P_1) would be:

$$P_1 = \frac{EV_0 + EV_0 \left(\frac{r_{wacc_0} - r_{wacc_1}}{r_{wacc_1}} \right) - D_1 + C_1}{S_1} = P_1$$

$$= \frac{EV_0 + EV_0 \left(\frac{r_{wacc_0} - r_{wacc_1}}{r_{wacc_1}} \right) - D_1 + C_1}{S_0 - \frac{\Delta D}{P_0}}$$

Assume the current price of the stock is $10\ SEK$, outstanding shares $100\ M$, $WACC$ 9%, current debts $400\ MSEK$ and cash $100\ MSEK$. The company decides to borrow an additional $200\ MSEK$ for buyback as they believe it would decrease the $WACC$ to 8%. The new stock price should be:

$$EV_0 = 1000 + 400 - 100 = 1300\ MSEK$$

$$P_1 = \frac{EV_0 + EV_0 \left(\frac{r_{wacc_0} - r_{wacc_1}}{r_{wacc_1}} \right) - D_1 + C_1}{S_0 - \frac{\Delta D}{P_0}}$$

$$= \frac{1300 + 1300 \left(\frac{0.09 - 0.08}{0.08} \right) - 600 + 100}{100 - \frac{200}{10}} = 12.03\ SEK$$

In some cases, it could be good as a shareholder to understand whether r_{wacc} has increased after the decision of new debts and buybacks to comprehend the efficiency of decision making conditioned on P_1, S_1 and so forth are known. The same equation can be used to solve for r_{wacc_1}:

$$P_1 = \frac{EV_0 + EV_0 \left(\frac{r_{wacc_0}}{r_{wacc_1}} - 1 \right) - D_1 + C_1}{S_1} = \frac{EV_0 + EV_0 \frac{r_{wacc_0}}{r_{wacc_1}} - EV_0 - D_1 + C_1}{S_1}$$

$$\Rightarrow P_1 * S_1 - C_1 + D_1 = EV_0 \frac{r_{wacc_0}}{r_{wacc_1}} \Rightarrow r_{wacc_1}(P_1 * S_1 - C_1 + D_1) = EV_0 * r_{wacc_0}$$

$$\Rightarrow r_{wacc_1} = \frac{EV_0 * r_{wacc_0}}{(P_1 * S_1 - C_1 + D_1)}$$

Assume from the example above that the firm borrows 400 MSEK instead, where r_{wacc_1} is unknown. After the firm has borrowed, it buys back shares (equivalent to the amount borrowed) at different buyback prices, managing to buy back 35 M shares. The new stock price is 9.5 SEK. It should be implicitly that the firm overestimated its forecast and (or) the prices it could buyback at as the stock price decreased, ceteris paribus:

$$r_{wacc_1} = \frac{EV_0 * r_{wacc_0}}{(P_1 * S_1 - C_1 + D_1)} = \frac{1300 * 0.09}{(9.5 * 35 - 100 + 800)} = 11.33\%$$

So far, it has been assumed that there is no growth associated with the business model, but let us implement a static growth:

$$\Delta EV_0 = \Delta \left(\frac{FCFE_1}{r_{wacc_0} - g} \right) = \frac{FCFE_1}{r_{wacc_1} - g} - \frac{FCFE_1}{r_{wacc_0} - g}$$

$$= FCFE_1 \left(\frac{1}{r_{wacc_1} - g} - \frac{1}{r_{wacc_0} - g} \right)$$

$$\Rightarrow FCFE_1 \left(\frac{r_{wacc_0} - r_{wacc_1}}{(r_{wacc_1} - g) * (r_{wacc_0} - g)} \right)$$

$$= EV_0 * (r_{wacc_0} - g) \left(\frac{r_{wacc_0} - r_{wacc_1}}{(r_{wacc_1} - g) * (r_{wacc_0} - g)} \right)$$

Leading to:

$$P_1 = \frac{EV_0 + EV_0 * (r_{wacc_0} - g) \left(\frac{r_{wacc_0} - r_{wacc_1}}{(r_{wacc_1} - g) * (r_{wacc_0} - g)} \right) - D_1 + C_1}{S_1}$$

The firm example above can be used and further assume that the growth of the firm is equal to the inflation of 2%, as it is large cap stock (common assumption):

$$P_1 = \frac{EV_0 + EV_0 * (r_{wacc_0} - g)\left(\frac{r_{wacc_0} - r_{wacc_1}}{(r_{wacc_1} - g)*(r_{wacc_0} - g)}\right) - D_1 + C_1}{S_1} = P_1$$

$$= \frac{1300 + 1300 * (0.09 - 0.02)\left(\frac{0.09 - 0.08}{(0.08 - 0.02)*(0.09 - 0.02)}\right) - 600 + 100}{100 - \frac{200}{10}}$$

$$= 12.71$$

And if solving for r_{wacc_1}:

$$P_1 * S_1 + D_1 - C_1 - EV_0 = EV_0 * (r_{wacc_0} - g)\frac{r_{wacc_0} - r_{wacc_1}}{(r_{wacc_1} - g)*(r_{wacc_0} - g)}$$

Multiply $(r_{wacc_1} - g)$ on both sides:

$$(P_1 * S_1 + D_1 - C_1 - EV_0) * (r_{wacc_1} - g) = EV_0 * (r_{wacc_0} - r_{wacc_1})$$

$$\Rightarrow (P_1 * S_1 + D_1 - C_1 - EV_0) * r_{wacc_1} - g * (P_1 * S_1 + D_1 - C_1 - EV_0) + EV_0$$
$$* r_{wacc_1} = EV_0 * r_{wacc_0}$$

$$\Rightarrow (P_1 * S_1 + D_1 - C_1 - EV_0) * r_{wacc_1} + EV_0 * r_{wacc_1}$$
$$= EV_0 * r_{wacc_0} + g * (P_1 * S_1 + D_1 - C_1 - EV_0)$$

$$\Rightarrow [(P_1 * S_1 + D_1 - C_1 - EV_0) + EV_0] * r_{wacc_1}$$
$$= EV_0 * r_{wacc_0} + g * (P_1 * S_1 + D_1 - C_1 - EV_0)$$

And finally:

$$r_{wacc_1} = \frac{EV_0 * r_{wacc_0} + g * (P_1 * S_1 + D_1 - C_1 - EV_0)}{P_1 * S_1 + D_1 - C_1}$$
$$= \frac{EV_0 * (r_{wacc_0} - g) + g * (P_1 * S_1 + D_1 - C_1)}{P_1 * S_1 + D_1 - C_1}$$

Using the examples above:

$$r_{wacc_1} = \frac{EV_0 * (r_{wacc_0} - g) + g * (P_1 * S_1 + D_1 - C_1)}{P_1 * S_1 + D_1 - C_1}$$

$$= \frac{1300 * (0.09 - 0.02) + 0.02 * \left[12.71 * \left(100 - \frac{200}{10}\right) + 600 - 100\right]}{12.71 * \left(100 - \frac{200}{10}\right) + 600 - 100} = 8\%$$

One should be aware that these two models might not always be accurate as it was assumed that the shareholder has access to the company internal data and assumptions (to estimate rather new price) or that the market participants can correctly price the new stock after the buybacks.

The impact of the financial statements after buybacks will be a decrease in cash and cash equivalents and equity (treasury stock). Treasury stock (TS) can be seen as the offset to common stock. As the company issues more stocks, an increase in share capital (SC) and cash and cash equivalents, the number of outstanding shares will increase. Hence, RIM could be adjusted as:

$$BE_t = NI_t + BE_{t-1} - D + SC - TS \Rightarrow D = NI_t + BE_{t-1} + SC_t - TS_t - BE_t$$

Where each of these variables are per share at their time period (as needed), adjusted for after the issuing and/or repurchases of shares. Using the same procedure:

$$P_0 = BE_0 + \sum_{t=1}^{\infty} \frac{NI_t - r_e * BE_{t-1} + SC_t - TS_t}{(1 + r_e)^t} + \frac{P_{\infty} - BE_{\infty}}{(1 + r_e)^{\infty}}$$

DDM is accustomed to being adjusted for treasury stock as it produces value to shareholders, improving ratios as EPS. The choice between using additional debts or cash and cash equivalents for repurchases will depend on how the discount rate would change, as if the company moves farther away from the optimal debt ratio or closer. Hence, adjusting DDM for treasury stock:

$$P_0 = \sum_{t=1}^{\infty} \frac{Div_t + TS_t}{(1 + r_e)^t} + \frac{P_{\infty}}{(1 + r_e)^{\infty}}$$

Would result in an adjusted RIM:

$$P_0 = BE_0 + \sum_{t=1}^{\infty} \frac{NI_t - r_e * BE_{t-1} + SC_t}{(1+r_e)^t} + \frac{P_\infty - BE_\infty}{(1+r_e)^\infty}$$

As:

$$D = NI_t + BE_{t-1} + SC_t - TS_t - BE_t \Rightarrow D + TS_t = NI_t + BE_{t-1} + SC_t - BE_t$$

The issuing of stocks could be for financing operations, as cash are brought into the firm at the selling of equity securities. As this happens, common stock increases with voting and cash flow rights. Companies could issue different classes of common stock (e.g., Class A and Class B) with different entitlement of their voting power. While issuing stocks could be as a form of financing, it could also occur as employees gets a compensation plan, stock option, or the usage of convertible bond. A convertible bond gives the bondholder the right to convert the bond into a pre-specified number of shares. The number of shares specified is call the conversation ratio (for instance, per $10\,000\,SEK$ bond $=$ 20 045 shares) which can be static or dynamic overt time. At the issuing of this bond, the ratio is set so that the value of the bond is greater than its conversation value (conversation ratio multiplied by the stock price). If this is the case at maturity, then the bondholder would choose to not convert and receive the nominal amount as any other bond retired at the maturity date. Employee stock options is a form of compensation plan, granting the employee the right to buy at a pre-specified price (exercise price) and shares at a pre-specified expiration date (a warrant for instance). If the employee chooses to exercise, conditioned on the exercise being greater than the price at the expiration date, the number of shares would increase (increasing common stocks by the exercise multiplied by the number of new shares). Both of these instruments results in the company being forced to issue more stocks. One problem with issuing additional shares, is the dilution of ownerships and cash flows. As outstanding shares increases, ratios as EPS decreases, ceteris paribus. Therefore, it is common that companies use repurchases of the stock to reset the increase.

Lerner & Auster (1969)[12] were interested in how the market reacts to potential earnings dilution. They measured the potential dilution as:

$$\left(\frac{\dfrac{P}{E_A} - \dfrac{P}{E_B}}{\dfrac{P}{E_B}} \right) * 100$$

E_A being earning per share after the conversation of debt and preferred stock takes place and E_B before that. Lerner & Auster used a sample of 164 U.S companies in 1967 which reported both current and diluted earnings and did not have an earnings deficit. Their results exhibited the greater the threat of future dilution, the greater the implied discount rate. The P/E_A for low dilution companies were greater compared to those with a high, implementing the market is willing to pay more for stocks with internally generated earnings than purchased (as issuing of stocks could also be used for acquisition and merger).

Dittmar (2000)[13] used a sample of firms from Compustat and the Center for Research in Security Prices (CRSP) between 1977-96, excluding financial institutions, public utilities and transportation companies as they were regulated under the period. The results exhibited that firms repurchased stock when it was considered to be undervalued, but also to distribute excess capital and alter leverage ratios. Further, Dittmar states that during mid-1980s, companies used repurchases to defend against takeover attempts while in the late 1980s and early 1990s repurchases were used to counter the effect of stock options. Kahle (2002)[14] argues that the sudden increase in repurchases in the early 1990s could not be of stocks being perceived as undervalued, concluded by previous studies. But agrees with Dittmar conclusion regarding the countereffect of stock options. Kahle examined how stock options affects the

---

[12] Lerner, E., & Auster, R. (1969). Does the Market Discount Potential Dilution. *Financial Analysts Journal, 25*(4), 118-121. Retrieved June 29, 2020, from www.jstor.org/stable/4470554

[13] Dittmar, A. (2000). Why Do Firms Repurchase Stock. *The Journal of Business, 73*(3), 331-355. doi:10.1086/209646

[14] Kahle, M, K. (2002), When a buyback isn't a buyback: open market repurchases and employee options, Journal of Financial Economics, 63, (2), 235-261

decision of repurchase between 1992-96. The results indicated that as compensation policy has changed, it caused a change in payout policy. Especially, for stock option, which have encouraged firm to repurchase shares as it does not affect the managerial options. Dividends does, as it causes a stock price decrease (conditioned on the option not containing any dividend protection).   Weisbenner (2004)[15] concluded in generic the increase in repurchases and decrease in earnings retention are associated with stock option program. While other studies have pointed the problem with dilution accounting for EPS, Weisbenner argues that stock option program could have the opposite effect or countereffect as the replacement of an increase in wages (direct cost) in proportion to options would lead to a decrease in expenses, boosting the reported earnings.

Grullon & Michaely (2002)[16] argue that taxes are a major component of the increase in repurchases as repurchases would not result being taxed at the ordinary income tax rate (like dividends). Further the approval of Rule 10b-18, decreasing the restrictions on repurchases should be considered as a major component as companies with a lot of repurchases could be charge by manipulation by SEC before Rule 10b-18. While effect of the taxation changed took time, the approval of Rule 10b-18 had an immediate effect where repurchases experienced an upward structural shift right after.

Root, Roztcki & Suh (2014)[17] analysed the net dilution (ND) on firm and industry level with a sample of 894 globally firms over 21 years ending in 2011. These firms are traded on the NASDAQ, NYSE or AMEX stock exchanges. Root, Roztcki & Suh defined the net dilution as:

---

[15] Weisbenner, S. (2004). Corporate Share Repurchases in the 1990s : What Role Do Stock Options Play?. Finance and Economics Discussion Series. 2000. 1-43. 10.17016/FEDS.2000.29.

[16] Grullon, G., & Michaely, R. (2002). Dividends, Share Repurchases, and the Substitution Hypothesis. The Journal of Finance, 57(4), 1649-1684. Retrieved June 29, 2020, from www.jstor.org/stable/3094520

[17] ROOT, T., ROZYCKI, J., & SUH, I. (2014). Share Repurchases and Long-term Dilution: Firm Characteristics and Industry Differences. *Quarterly Journal of Finance and Accounting, 52*(3/4), 1-51. Retrieved June 29, 2020, from www.jstor.org/stable/24634451

$$\left(\frac{portionate\ increase\ in\ total\ market}{portionate\ increase\ in\ the\ stock\ price}\right) * 100 = ND$$

Where:

$$ND > 100 = increase, \qquad ND < 100 = decrease$$

As an example, assume the market value of firm's equity would increase from 1000 MSEK to 1100 MSEK, with an outstanding share of 100 M, increasing the stock price from 10 SEK to 11 SEK. As for the compensation, management has 10 stock options at an exercise price of 10 SEK. At the expiration date, the increase in shares would be 10 M (outstanding shares equal to 110 M) while the market value of equity would increase by 100 MSEK (10 M * 10 SEK). This increase in shares and market value would result in a decrease of the stock price to 10.91 SEK (1200/110). Then:

$$ND = \left(\frac{\frac{1200}{1000}}{\frac{10.91}{10}}\right) * 100 = 110$$

The dilution of ownership, as the shareholders' ownership weakened, may not be realised as the stock price increased. The results revealed that high diluters experience a compounded annual net dilution rate of 5.5%. As for low diluters, they experience a compounded annual net dilution rate of approximately - 0.8%. High diluters consisted of utilities, energy, financials and technology industries while consumer staples are the solitary non-diluting industry. While high diluters experience a greater growth in assets and sales, than low diluters, Root, Roztcki & Suh argues that this could have an adverse reaction as high diluters would have lower profitability, dividends, turnover and price to book ratio despite greater leverage and systematic risk.

2.7 Which method is superior?

While these different methods, discussed, have its advantages, the DCF method is mostly favoured by finance literature as it is unaffected by accounting methods[18]. But both RI and DCF are theoretical equivalent, meaning they should both yield an identical firm value estimate. According to Ohlson (1995)[19] if clean surplus accounting is applied, the RI method would be insensitive to different accounting methods. Clean surplus accounting means that several unrealised posts should be lifted in the income statement. For European listed companies, it is de facto after the first January 2009, according to IAS 1. Levin & Olsson (1998)[20] stated that as simplified assumptions were introduce, such for growth and terminal value, it would result bias in the firm value estimates. In their later research[21], year 2000, they demonstrated that if the steady state condition was not fulfilled, meaning the company was not stable after the calculated terminal value, the RI would yield a more accurate firm value than DCF.

To quantify, Bernard (1995)[22] found that RI explained approximately 68 percent of the stock price, when a 4-year forecast data were used, while if dividends were discounted, it only explained 29 percent. Earnings and residual income were found to be more informative than cash flow in Biddle, Bowen &

---

[18] Copeland, T., Koller, T., & Murrin, J. (1990). Valuation: Measuring and managing the value of companies. New York: Wiley

[19] Ohlson, J. (1995). Earnings, book values, and dividends in equity valuation. Contemporary Accounting Research, 661–687.

[20] Levin, J., & Olsson, P. (1998). Company valuation with a periodically adjusted cost of capital, published. In: Olsson, P. (Ed.), Studies in company valuation, Stockholm School of Economics

[21] Levin, J., & Olsson, P. (2000). Terminal value techniques in equity valuation implications of the steady state assumption. Research Report, Stockholm School of Economics, The Economic Research Institute

[22] Bernard, V. L. (1995). The Feltham-Ohlson framework: Implications for empiricists. Contemporary Accounting Research, 733–747.

Wallace (1997)[23] research. It was argued by Bernard (1989)[24] that the problem with cash flow is that a positive cash flow can be both positive and bad depending on the reason why it is positive, same for the opposite. Remember that these models need to be customized based on the business model. For instance, Forester & Sápp (2005)[25] collected 120 years of data on a single company, Bank of Montreal, to test the accuracy of DDM (with a two-stage model) as Bank of Montreal have had uninterrupted distribution of dividends. The results suggested that both DDM and the Gordon growth model (growing perpetuity model) performed well to explain the observed stock price.

According to Thomas's (2002)[26] results, DCF is more sensitive to simplified growth assumption than RI as RI uses what has already been provided by the company in its financial (FCFE and FCFF are not displayed as net income, EBIT, book equity etc). Therefore, RI places less reliance on the terminal value (forecasts are easier accessible) than DCF and would generate an accurate firm value estimate (than DCF) when simplified growth assumption is introduced. According to Plenborg (1996)[27], time series patterns of earnings were more stable. Further, Dechow, Kothari & Watts (1998)[28] results exhibit that current cash flow is less reliable than current earnings to forecast future cash flow.

---

[23] Biddle, G. C., Bowen, R. M., & Wallace, J. S. (1997). Does EVA beat earnings? Evidence on associations with stock returns and firm values. Journal of Accounting and Economics, 301–336

[24] Bernard, V. L. (1989). Capital markets research in accounting during the 1980s: A critical review. Working paper, University of Michigan.

[25] Foerster, S.R., & Sápp, S.G. (2005). The Dividend Discount Model in the Long-Run: A Clinical Study.

[26] Plenborg, Thomas. (2002). Firm valuation: Comparing the residual income and discounted cash flow approaches. Scandinavian Journal of Management. 18. 303-318. 10.1016/S0956-5221(01)00017-3.

[27] Plenborg, T. (1996). The information content of accrual and cash flow based performance measuresFfrom a Danish and US perspective. Ph.D. dissertation, Copenhagen Business School.

[28] Dechow, P., Kothari, S. P., & Watts, R. L. (1998). The relation between earnings and cash flows. Journal of Accounting and Economics, 133–168.

Francis, Olsson & Oswald (2000)[29] compared the DDM, DCF and RIM (two-stage models, terminal value after year 5) about their accuracy (difference between the stock price and the estimated) and explainability (ability to explain he cross-sectional variation in current stock prices). Francis et al. used a sample between 554 and 607 firms per year (large cap, listed on either the NYSE, AMEX or NASDAQ) from 1989-93 (2907 observations in the pooled sample). Their results suggested that, regarding the accuracy, RIM was superior compared to DCF and DDM. RIM had a prediction error of 30%, while DCF and DDM had a prediction error of 41% and 69%. As for the explainability, RIM explained, on average, 71% of the variation in stock prices, while DCF and DDM explained only, on average, 35% and 51%. As previously mentioned, RIM places a lower weight on the terminal value compared to DCF and DDM. Francis et al. results further indicated that the book value of equity represented on average 72% of the RIM estimates. The terminal value composed of approximately 21% of RIM estimates while for DCF and DDM it was 82% and 65% on average. While it has been argued that different accounting practices and polices might affect the accuracy of RIM, Francis et al. results suggested that the reliability of RIM remained unaffected whether it was accounting discretion or accounting conservatism applied, which supports the RIM is robust to the differences in accounting practices and policies. Lastly, Francis et al concluded that whether forecasted data or realised data were used, RIM would still had remained as the superior choice compared to DCF and DDM.

Reis & Augusto (2013) [30] brought up a challenge regarding all models that used the terminal value (perpetuity model) as a component. As the terminal value is used, it assumes that the company will continue to operate forever. But Reis & Augusto argues that the terminal value might be a problem as data from Coface Mope database shows that the average life expectancy of a company is

[29] Francis, J., Olsson, P., & Oswald, D. (2000). Comparing the Accuracy and Explainability of Dividend, Free Cash Flow, and Abnormal Earnings Equity Value Estimates. *Journal of Accounting Research, 38*(1), 45-70. doi:10.2307/2672922

[30] Nogueira Reis, Pedro & Augusto, Mário. (2013). The Terminal Value (TV) Performing in Firm Valuation: The Gap of Literature and Research Agenda. Journal of Accounting, Auditing and Finance. 9. 1622-1636.

12 years with a standard deviation of 11 years. The maximum years was 169. Coface Mope comprehends 242 661 records on insolvencies, dissolutions and ceasing of activity in Portugal from 1900 to April 2012. Indirectly, as the terminal value is incorporated, it excludes how crisis would condition the company's value. This only regards valuation of the whole firm. But what about the terminal value accounting for the shareholders? Rojo-Ramírez, Martínez-Romero & Mariño-Garrido (2017)[31] used a sample of 62 Spanish listed companies from 2005. They formed two hypothesis, the first, *"The implied terminal value (ITV) of the equity comprises the expectations of long-term value reflected in the equity terminal value (EqTV)"*, and the second, *"The Implied Terminal value (ITV) assigned by the market comprises the possible variations of the equity terminal value (EqTV) calculated through discounted cash flow model"*, where the implied terminal value is the difference between the enterprise value and the discounting cash flows. By running a multiple regression, with control variables, Rojo-Ramírez et al. results supports both the hypothesis as the equity terminal value exhibit to correlate positively and significantly with ITV and with the implied terminal value ratio (ITVR, ITV divided with the market value of shares). Therefore, the market takes the terminal value (of equity) into consideration, making it as an important variable in the models. However, Rojo-Ramírez et al. encourages that this should also be tested on larger samples.

It is feasible to believe that RIM is superior to DDM but notice when these studies were issued. As known, DDM was used to derive the RIM, so, theoretically they should provide an equivalent valuation estimate. Most of these studies were conducted before the new implementation of IAS 1 as, previously, the deviation could be of the violation of the clean surplus relation or an inconsistent growth rate. If surplus relation holds (as it should from 2009) then if the firm decides to pay less dividends, the growth rate should increase in its proportion as the growth is defined as the retention rate multiplied with the ROE (this can be amended based on assumptions). It is suspected that

[31] Rojo-Ramírez, A. & Martínez-Romero, M. J. & Mariño-Garrido, T.. (2017). How the Equity Terminal Value Influences the Value of the Firm?. Journal of Business Valuation and Economic Loss Analysis. 10.1515/jbvela-2017-0010.

either clean surplus relation is violated, or the wrong growth rate has been applied. Lundholm & Terry already in 2001[32] raised these concerns. They argued that there have been three error from these articles that states RIM being the superior. First is the inconsistent forecasts error, using a perpetuity model with the wrong amount. The second is the incorrect discount rate error, arising when valuing the whole firm first before quantifying the equity. The problem is the WACC, where the average weights only hold under certain conditions, as the weights, themselves, are not arbitrary. The third is the missing cash flow error, arising from the error of assuming clean surplus relation. Theoretically, RIM and DDM should generate the same estimate, given the CSI holds and no repurchase of shares or issues of shares happen. For instance, assume following values

	$t = 1$	$t = 2$	$t = 3$	$E(P_4)$
SE_{t-1}	3.25	3.8	4.3	50
NI_t	0.75	1	2	
D_t	0.2	0.5	1	
SE_t	3.8	4.3	5.3	

Where:

$$SE_t = NI_t - D_t + SE_{t-1}$$

Assuming a discount rate of 10%:

$$RIM = BE_{t-1} \sum_{t=1}^{T=3} \frac{NI_t - r_e BE_{t-1}}{(1 + r_e)^t} + \frac{E(P_4) - BE_T}{(1 + r_e)^T}$$

$$= 3.25 + \frac{0.75 - 0.1 * 3.25}{(1 + 0.1)^1} + \frac{0.75 - 0.1 * 3.8}{(1 + 0.1)^2} + \frac{0.75 - 0.1 * 4.3}{(1 + 0.1)^3}$$

$$+ \frac{50 - 5.3}{(1 + 0.1)^3} = 38.91$$

---

[32] Lundholm, Russell J. and Terry O'keefe (2001). "Reconciling Value Estimates from the Discounted Cash Flow Model and Residual Income Model." Contemporary Accounting Research. 18(2 (Summer)): 311-35.

$$DDM = \sum_{t=1}^{T=3} \frac{D_t}{(1+r_e)^t} + \frac{E(P_4)}{(1+r_e)^T}$$

$$= \frac{0.2}{(1+0.1)^1} + \frac{0.5}{(1+0.1)^2} + \frac{1}{(1+0.1)^3} + \frac{50}{(1+0.1)^3} = 38.91$$

The significant problem with this is the estimation of the terminal value. Since:

$$RIM = BE_{t-1} \sum_{t=1}^{T=\infty} \frac{NI_t - r_e BE_{t-1}}{(1+r_e)^t} = S_0 + \frac{NI_1 - r_e BE_0}{r_e} = \frac{NI_1}{r_e}$$

$$DDM = \sum_{t=1}^{T=\infty} \frac{D_t}{(1+r_e)^t} + \frac{E(P_4)}{(1+r_e)^T} = \frac{D_1}{r_e}$$

Mohammad (2012)[33] stated this problem to be a void in the transversality condition (no endpoint). For the model of RIM to hold, based on the assumptions made to structure the model, at the terminal value, the net income needs to be theoretically distributed as dividends:

$$\frac{D_1}{r_e} = \frac{NI_1}{r_e} \Rightarrow D_1 = \frac{NI_1}{r_e} r_e = NI_1$$

Or DDM will underestimate the stock price. Therefore, add another variable "ER" as for error, that is needed to equal the difference between the net income and dividends:

$$\frac{D_1 + ER_1}{r_e} = \frac{NI_1}{r_e}$$

Further, if the terminal value was to be estimated at a later date, then the error would change to:

$$\frac{D_{t+1} + ER_{t+1}}{r_e} \frac{1}{(1+r_e)^t} = \frac{NI_{t+1} - r_e BE_t}{r_e} \frac{1}{(1+r_e)^t} \Rightarrow D_{t+1} + ER_{t+1} = NI_{t+1} - r_e BE_t$$

---

[33] Mohammad, T. (2012). 'Is Residual Income Model (RIM) REALLY Superior to Dividend Discount Model (DDM)?' – A Misconception. IOSR Journal of Business and Management. 5. 36-44. 10.9790/487X-0563644.

$$\Rightarrow ER_{t+1} = NI_{t+1} - r_e BE_t - D_{t+1}$$

This is an adjustment that is not thought about from the articles stating RIM being the superior model. Before the implementation of IAS in 2009, Kämpe & Morin (2011) found that the dirty surplus account flow (the changes in capital that is not considered in the income statement, resulting in a violation of the CSI), has been significant for the large cap listed companies in Sweden from 2005 to 2009. So, it should not be a surprise that research prior 2009 got different estimates of RIM and DDM. Also, by adding the void that's created by the transversality condition, the models become more separated.

Recall adjustments of the models should be done towards the characteristic of the stock. It would not be sound to use a DDM for a stock that does not contain a good history of distributing dividends (if anything). If dealing with a bank who does not pay any dividends, RIM would be a better approach as it can be suspected that the free cash flow will be volatile (due to the business model).

There is mixed research on whether EVA is superior as Stephen (1996) claimed. As a matter of fact, EVA relies on generally accepted accounting principles (GAAP) issued by Financial Accounting Standards Board (FASB). GAAP is a set of recommendations which are not forced by law (in USA), except for listed companies where Securities and Exchange Commission (SEC) requires listed companies to follow GAAP. Hence, when EVA is used, some adjustments, stated by Stephen (1996), are needed. Some examples are research and development expenditures, and employee training costs, which should be capitalized and amortized over their perceived years of future benefits. The main difficulty with the implementation of EVA, is the calculated discount rate, where WACC is commonly used (Abdeen & Haight, 2002)[34]. Stewart in 1991,[35] published its book "The Quest for Value" where Stewart expressed its views about the usefulness of EVA. He collected a sample of 613

---

[34] Abdeen, A. M., & Haight, G. T. (2002). A Fresh Look At Economic Value Added: Empirical Study Of The Fortune Five-Hundred Companies. Journal of Applied Business Research (JABR), 18(2). https://doi.org/10.19030/jabr.v18i2.2112

[35] Stewart, G. B., III., The Quest for Value: The EVA® Management Guide (New York: Harper Business, 1991).

American companies and compared the 1984-85 and 1987-88. The conclusion was that there was a strong correlation between the EVA and MVA (Market Value Added) (R^2 of about 97%) but companies with negative EVA had a lesser correlation. Studies as Dodd & Chen (1996)[36], Biddle, Bowen & Wallace (1997)[37] have received contradictory results. Dodd & Chen had a sample of 566 American companies for the period 1986-92 where the results disclosed that EVA explained only 20% of the variability of the stock returns. Biddle et al results, for a period of 1983-94, suggested that earnings before extraordinary items had greater explanatory power of stock returns than EVA. Peixoto (2002)[38] tested EVA for 39 Portuguese companies for the period 1995–98. Net income had a higher informational content than EVA but when MVA acted as the dependent variable, than EVA disclosed to have the greatest informational content. Dimitris & Christos (2007)[39] used a sample of 121 non-financial publicly traded Greek firms from 1996 to 2003. Their results did not support Stern Stewart's claims that EVA is more correlated with stock market returns. As with Peixoto, the net income exhibit to have the greatest relative information content. In line with my opinions, Dimitris & Christos argue that the deviations could be because of the underlying assumptions to estimate WACC. Other explanations, provided by Dimitris & Christos, are the adjustments proposed by Stern Stewart, the majority of investors (Greek) did not regard the economic profit measures as the importance of estimating the total cost of capital and other variables were not recognise, lastly stock returns are more a result of the dynamics of the market's pectations for the firm's future cash flows.

---

[36] Chen, S. and Dodd, J. L. (1998). 'Usefulness of operating income, residual income and EVA: a value-relevance perspective', Working Paper (Clarion University and Drake University).

[37] Biddle, G. C., Bowen, R. and Wallace, J. S. (1997). 'Does EVA beat earnings? Evidence on associations with stock returns and firm values', Journal of Accounting and Economics, Vol. 24, no. 3, pp. 301–36.

[38] Peixoto, S. (2002). 'Economic value added: an application to Portuguese public companies', Working Paper (Moderna University of Porto).

[39] Dimitris, K & Christos, A. (2007). The Validity of the Economic Value Added Approach: an Empirical Application. European Financial Management. 13. 71 - 100. 10.1111/j.1468-036X.2006.00286.x.

Still, Dimitris & Christos remain positive that EVA could have a great impact on the Greek listed companies as Greek stock market becomes more mature and stable. Personally, I would argue that the main problem is the WACC for why there are different conclusions regarding the explanation power of EVA. Further, in some research, EVA could be defined as:

$$EVA = NOPAT - r_{wacc} * EV$$

Instead of lagging EV by one period, a different (and severe) result will be retrieved:

$$NOPAT - r_{wacc} * EV = NOPAT - \left(\frac{ME}{EV} r_e + \frac{MD}{EV} r_{dMD} (1 - t_c) \right) EV$$

$$= NOPAT - MEr_e + MDr_{dMD}(1 - t_c) = Net\ income - MEr_e$$

If ME was replaced with its book value (of equity), then the problem can be seen (which model is it if you lag the book value of equity by one period?).

2.8 Summary

As illustrated, the modifications of the predefined models in ch.1 deviate conditional on the choice of cash flows. While the theoretical value should not differ as the fundamentals remain identical, it does so in practice. However, with an increase of accounting regulations, this discrepancy should be mitigated (eliminated if so). Hence, not only should the decision of cash flow be subjective to the firm's characteristics, but also its transparency and the ease of accounting regulation.

Questions for chapter 2

1. With an expected income of 10 MSEK, retention rate of 70% and change of debt by 5 MSEK, what is the expected FCFE for year 1?
2. By reading the Morningstar key ratios for stock A, following information were retrieved:

In MSEK	2018 (0)
CFOA	100
Interest expenses	6
CAPEX	20
Debts issued	35.4
Debts paid	50

Calculate both FCFE and FCFF for year 0 assuming a tax rate of 20%. Thereafter, estimate the stock price for stock A with an expected growth of 1%, discount rate by 7% and outstanding shares of 4 MSEK, assuming stock A remains in a stable condition.

3. What is the implied $FCFE_0$ per share given a stock price of 10 SEK, growth of 1.5% and discount rate of 6% assuming the company is in a stable condition?

4. Assume following values:

In MSEK	Year 0
EV	1000
Interest expenses	9
WACC	8%
g	2%
Debts issued	10
Debts paid	20.5
r_e	10%
Outstanding shares	2
t_c	35%

Calculate what the stock price should be assuming a growing perpetuity model. A hint would be to think of you first can retrieve FCFF by EV and thereafter FCFE from FCFF.

5. With the following values, calculate the stock price:

In MSEK	Year 1	Year 2	Year 3
CFOA	100	150	120
Interest expenses	6	9	7
CAPEX	20	25	23
Debts issued	35.4	20	25
Debts paid	50	30	25
Outstanding shares	2	2	2
r_e	10%	10%	8%

Where at year 3, the firm is assumed to be in a stable condition.

6. What should the stock price be with the following values:

In MSEK	Year 0	Year 1	Year 2	Year 3 (steady state)
NI	500	600	625	800
BE	5500	6000	6600	7225
r_e	0.09	0.09	0.09	0.06
Outstanding shares	15	15	15	15

7. If the FCFF is expected to result in 120 MSEK in year 1, with outstanding shares of 4M, cash of 10 MSEK, debts 50 MSEK, WACC of 7% and growth of 0.5%, what should the stock price be? A hint is to first estimate what the EV Should be and thereafter decompose its components to derive the stock price.

8. What is the expected stock price after the buybacks given an EV_0 of 1000 MSEK, $WACC_0$ and $WACC_1$ of 7% and 5%, cash of 30 MSEK, debts of 300 MSEK, outstanding shares of 200 M, P_0 of 20 SEK and increase in debts for the buybacks of 200 MSEK?

2.9 Appendix

2.9.1 The usage of Comparable valuation

Generic, analysts prefer to use multiples to describe the attractiveness of a stock as one "avoid" the assumptions by DCF, DDM, RIM etc. But, using multiples as P/E will only make these assumptions implicit. Recall for a growing perpetuity model:

$$P_0 = \frac{Div_0(1+g)}{r-g}$$

Where it is known that:

$$\frac{Div_0}{NI_0} = payout$$

Hence:

$$\frac{P_0}{NI_0} = \frac{payout_0(1+g)}{r-g} = P/E$$

This can also be applied for a two stage:

$$P_0 = \frac{Div_1}{r-g}\left(1 - \frac{(1+g)^n}{(1+r)^n}\right) + \frac{\frac{Div_{n+1}}{r_{n+1} - g_{n+1}}}{(1+r)^n}$$

$$\Rightarrow \frac{P_0}{NI_0} = \frac{payout_0(1+g)}{r-g}\left(1 - \frac{(1+g)^n}{(1+r)^n}\right) + \frac{\frac{payout_{n+1}}{r_{n+1} - g_{n+1}}}{(1+r)^n}$$

The drawback for using multiples as a valuation arises at its core usage, the comparison. P/E does not describe any significantly if not comparing it to similar companies. As established, a high P/E can implicate the nominator being significantly greater or the denominator lesser. It is of higher probability that the denominator is dynamic (or greater) compared to the nominator as discount rate integrate the expectation of the risk premium. Therefore, the denominator might be the cause of a high (or low) multiple. If an analyst uses P/E from two similar companies to compute their stock price:

$$P/E_A = P/E_B \Rightarrow P_A = P/E_B * E_A$$

$$P/E_A = P/E_B \Rightarrow P_B = P/E_A * E_B$$

Could be inaccuracy if the sector is overvalued (high multiplies), implicating low discount rates (from the deduction). The computation of other multiples is similar to P/E, a growing perpetuity model for P/BV and P/S:

$$\frac{P_0}{BV_0} = \frac{1}{BV_0} \frac{EPS_0 * payout_0(1+g)}{r-g} = \frac{ROE_0 * payout_0(1+g)}{r-g}$$

$$\frac{P_0}{Sales} = \frac{1}{Sales} \frac{EPS_0 * payout_0(1+g)}{r-g} = \frac{Net\ margin_0 * payout_0(1+g)}{r-g}$$

Two-stage model:

$$\frac{P_0}{BV_0} = \frac{1}{BV_0} \frac{EPS_0 * payout_0(1+g)}{r-g}\left(1 - \frac{(1+g)^n}{(1+r)^n}\right)$$

$$+ \frac{1}{BV_0} \frac{\frac{EPS_0 * payout_0(1+g)(1+g)^n}{r_{n+1} - g_{n+1}}}{(1+r)^n}$$

$$= \frac{ROE_0 * payout_0(1+g)}{r-g}\left(1 - \frac{(1+g)^n}{(1+r)^n}\right) + \frac{\frac{ROE_0 * payout_0(1+g)(1+g)^n}{r_{n+1} - g_{n+1}}}{(1+r)^n}$$

$$\frac{P_0}{Sales} = \frac{1}{Sales} \frac{EPS_0 * payout_0(1+g)}{r-g}\left(1 - \frac{(1+g)^n}{(1+r)^n}\right)$$

$$+ \frac{1}{Sales} \frac{\frac{EPS_0 * payout_0(1+g)(1+g)^n}{r_{n+1} - g_{n+1}}}{(1+r)^n}$$

$$= \frac{Net\ margin_0 * payout_0(1+g)}{r-g}\left(1 - \frac{(1+g)^n}{(1+r)^n}\right)$$

$$+ \frac{\frac{Net\ margin_0 * payout_0(1+g)(1+g)^n}{r_{n+1} - g_{n+1}}}{(1+r)^n}$$

Fielitz & Frederick (1985)[40] compared multiples as P/E and dividend yield with a model that incorporates these multiples together added with other objectives in a two-stage model. Fielitz & Frederick specified the price of a stock as:

$$P_0 = \frac{NI_0(1+g_1)(1-b_1)}{(1+r_1)} + \frac{NI_1(1+g_2)(1-b_2)}{(1+r_1)(1+r_2)} + \cdots$$

b being the retention rate and r the discount rate. Fielitz & Frederick criticise the model as it requires projections about the growth rate, discount rate and payout. As they assume the rates being continuously compounded, they integrated the model;

$$P_0 = \int_0^n NI_0(1-b_1)e^{n(g-r)} + P_n e^{-rn} = NI_0 \left(\frac{(1-b)e^{n*risk\,factor}}{risk\,factor} + \frac{e^{n*risk\,factor}}{r} \right)$$

Where:

$$\frac{P_0}{P} = \frac{NI_0}{P} \left(\frac{(1-b)e^{n*risk\,factor}}{risk\,factor} + \frac{e^{n*risk\,factor}}{r} \right)$$

Be aware that P is the de facto stock price while P_0 is the theoretical stock price (intrinsic value). Fielitz & Frederick used a time horizon of 5 years in the first stage. Further, it is assumed that $g = ROE * b = r * b$ since they assumed $r = ROE$. Multiplying P on LHS and RHS (inside the barracks):

$$P_0 = \frac{NI_0}{P} \left(\frac{(1-b)e^{n*risk\,factor}}{risk\,factor} + \frac{e^{n*risk\,factor}}{r} \right) P$$

$$= \frac{NI_0}{P} \left(\frac{g_5 100}{risk\,factor} + \frac{\frac{DIV_5}{P} * 100}{risk\,factor} \right) = \frac{g_5 100 + \frac{DIV_5}{P} * 100}{\frac{P/NI_0}{risk\,factor}}$$

$$= \frac{NI_0 \left(g_5 100 + \frac{DIV_5}{P} * 100 \right)}{P * risk\,factor}$$

[40] Fielitz, B., & Frederick L. Muller. (1985). A Simplified Approach to Common Stock Valuation. Financial Analysts Journal, 41(6), 35-41. Retrieved June 18, 2020, from www.jstor.org/stable/4478883

Lastly, Fielitz & Frederick argued that for the ease of analysis without losing substance, they assumed the expected dividends in year 5 to be equal to year 1. Further, as the coming year net income is of more interest than the current, the current net income is replaced with the one in year 1. Hence:

$$P_0 = \frac{\frac{g_5 100 + \frac{DIV_1}{P} * 100}{P/NI_1}}{risk\ factor}$$

The results suggested this model to be superior compared to each component themselves, specially P/E and DIV/P. However, P/E exhibit abnormal returns as low P/E outperformed the ones with high. Nicholson (1960)[41] and McWilliams (1966)[42] agree that low P/E has a greater probability of abnormal returns than those with a high. According to Nicholson, high P/E can be a reflection of investor satisfaction with companies of high quality, triggering an increase in the stock price relative to the earnings. However, as these often runs to extremes, they become subject to slow-down or reversal. Tobias E. Carlisle defined this phenomenon as "mean reversion" in his book *"Deep Value: Why Activist Investors and Other Contrarians Battle for Control of Losing Corporations"*.

There is a phenomenon called *Value Trap*[43]. Stocks with low P/E (high E/P) are considered as value stocks and high P/E (low E/P) as growth stocks. But some stocks might deserve a lesser P/E and should therefore not be considered as of value. From a growing perpetuity model where net income per share in year 1 is of interest:

$$P_0 = \frac{NI_1}{r_e - g} \Rightarrow \frac{NI_1}{P_0} = r_e - g$$

---

[41] S. Francis Nicholson. (1960). Price-Earnings Ratios. *Financial Analysts Journal, 16*(4), 43-45. Retrieved June 18, 2020, from www.jstor.org/stable/4469053

[42] James D. McWilliams. (1966). Prices, Earnings and P-E Ratios. Financial Analysts Journal, 22(3), 137-142. Retrieved June 18, 2020, from www.jstor.org/stable/4470000

[43] Penman S. H., Reggiani F. (2018). Fundamentals of Value versus Growth Investing and an Explanation for the Value Trap, Financial Analysts Journal, 74(4), pp. 103-119.

The forward price to earnings would increase due to the increase in the discount rate or decrease due to the increase in growth. The problem that arises is whether the growth is risky, meaning that an increase in growth implies a greater discount rate. Then a stock with a high E/P (low P/E) could just be of a high discount rate and growth which should be classified as a growth stock rather than a value stock. Penman & Reggiani used B/P to illustrates this phenomenon:

$$\frac{BE_0}{P_0} = \frac{BE_0}{NI_1}\frac{NI_1}{P_0} = \frac{BE_0}{NI_1}(r_e - g)$$

Notice that $\frac{BE_0}{NI_1}$ is the inverse of ROE, therefore this can be rewritten as:

$$\frac{P_0}{BE_0} = \frac{ROE}{(r_e - g)}$$

A lower price to book value could either be because of a lower ROE, higher growth conditioned on a low ROE implies a higher expected growth rate or if a higher growth rate is associated with a higher discount rate. Growth is considered to be a delayment of the recognition of earnings which ties it to risk. But delaying earnings also lowers the ROE. Therefore, an increase in ROE could imply that earnings are being realized, lowering the risk. But, this can contradictory as:

$$ROE = \frac{NI_0}{BE_0} = \frac{NI_0}{Revenue}\frac{Revenue}{TA}\frac{TA}{BE_0}$$

So:

$$\frac{P_0}{BE_0} = \frac{\frac{NI_0}{Revenue}\frac{Revenue}{TA}\frac{TA}{BE_0}}{(r_e - g)}$$

If the ROE has decreased over the years, due to a decrease in TA/BE_0, ceteris paribus, then a lower ROE would not necessarily mean that the risk has increased, maybe the opposite. Therefore, it is not as easy as one could think. If the theorical price is greater than the actual, it does not necessarily mean the stock is undervalued. This requires time series of the different components to understand what the underlying problem could be. A higher Price to Book multiple could imply that net margin has increased, which is positive rather than if equity multiplier had.

A growing perpetuity dividend model can be further used to show the importance[44]:

$$P_0 = \frac{Div_1}{r_e - g} = \frac{NI_1 * payout}{r_e - g}$$

Where

$$\frac{P_0}{NI_1} = \frac{payout}{r_e - g} = \frac{1}{r_e} + \frac{(ROE - r_e)}{r_e} \frac{(1 - payout)}{r_e - g}$$

This relationship describes the reason why the forward P/E would be low could be because of the stock's low ROE to its r_e, low growth, low reinvestment value or high perception of risk on future earnings. Even with this relationship, it requires a time series analysis of these components. Therefore, one should be cautioned to choose stocks with low multiplies as it is unknown at first what the cause of that could be.

It is not meant to discourage the usage of comparable valuation, quite the opposite. But it entails that caution should be taken as low multiples could indicate more than what is thought conventional.

2.9.2 EPRA NAV IAS 40 & IFRS 13

EPRA NAV includes the NAV with adjustment to the fair value of properties and other investment interests and to exclude items that are not expected to crystallise in a long-term investment property business model. This makes IAS 40 and IFRS 13 of interest as IAS 40 regulates the definition of an investment property and IFRS 13 discloses the measurement of fair value. IAS 40 defines an investment property as

---

[44] Pinochi, Marco and Fais, Fabio and Corsiglia, Marco, Residual Income Model and Abnormal Returns: A Comparison to Factor Styles and Sell-Side Analysts (June 25, 2019). Business Valuation OIV Journal Spring 2019. Available at SSRN: https://ssrn.com/abstract=3478213 or http://dx.doi.org/10.2139/ssrn.3478213

"Investment property is property (land or a building or part of a building or both) held (by the owner or by the lessee under a finance lease) to earn rentals or for capital appreciation or both."

When this is fulfilled, an investment property can be recognised as an asset when *"it is probable that the future economic benefits that are associated with the property will flow to the entity, and the cost of the property can be reliably measured"* (IAS 40.16). As IAS 40 got criticized for its ability regarding the subjectivity of fair value measurement, IFRS 13 was issued in 2013 (Marton, Lundqvist, Lumsden & Peterson, 2013)[45]. IFRS 13 defines the fair value as

"The price that would be received to sell an asset or paid to transfer a liability in an orderly transaction between market participants at the measurement date"

As it can be difficult in different market to retrieved what the market price would be, IFRS splits the measurement into three different levels:

1. Level I: *"are quoted prices in active markets for identical assets or liabilities that the entity can access at the measurement date"*
2. Level II: *"are inputs other than quoted market prices included within Level 1 that are observable for the asset or liability, either directly or indirectly"*
3. Level III: *"are unobservable inputs for the asset or liability"*

The usage of the levels depends on the data provided. If there are no active market, level 2 should be chosen. But if there are no observable data available, then assumptions and internal judgments will be used (level 3). Further, IFRS has stated characteristics such as relevance, reliability, comparability and consistency to improve the quality of financial information. The reason why it is important to have a certain knowledge of this, is that, it has been supported by several studies that companies tend to manage their earnings to show a

---

[45] Marton, J., Lundqvist, P., Lumsden, M. & Peterson, A-K. (2013). IFRS – i teori och praktik. Uppl. 3. Stockholm: Bonnier Utbildning.

desirable performance (Healy & Wahlen, 1999; Jaggi & Leung, 2003; Landsman, 2007; Dietrich, Harris, & Muller II, 2001)[46].

Simunovic & Wennergren (2015)[47] results suggested, for Swedish real estate companies, the investment properties are on average sold at 13.6 % above the booked value, which questions the reliability aspect. Also, if there is a bonus plan, then managers choose to value their property higher. Further, concentrated ownership affects the sales negatively if there is a bonus plan. Last, capital structure has a positive effect on sales. Gustafsson & Peng (2016)[48] conducted a study on 14 Swedish listed real estate companies from 2008 to 2015 with the aim to see what drive, impact and influence the discount/premium. Their results suggested that market sentiment, measured as the overall market discount rate and volatility significantly affected the NAV positively while size of the company, its portfolio focus, debt ratio and reputation had a significantly negative effect on the NAV. This means that variables as overall market discount rate and volatility increase the discount to NAV as they increase while variables as size of the company, its portfolio focus (focused property portfolio), debt ratio (total debt divided by the total assets) and reputation (return) decrease the discount to NAV as they increase.

[46] Healy P. & Wahlen, J. (1999). A Review of the Earnings Management Literature and Its Implications for Standard Setting. *Accounting Horizonz*, 13 (4), 365-383.

Jaggi, B. & Leung, S. (2003). Choice of accounting method for valuation of investment securities: evidence from Hong Kong firms. *Journal of International Financial Management and Accounting*. 14(2), 115-145.

Landsman, W. (2007). Is fair value accounting information relevant and reliable? Evidence from Journal of Economic Perspectives, 24 (1), 93-118

Dietrich, J.R., Harris, M.S., & Muller III, K.A. (2001). The reliability of investment property fair value estimates. Journal of Accounting and Economics, 30, 125-158.

[47] Simunovic, J., & Wennergren, J. (2015). The Reliability of Fair Value in Investment Property. a study on Swedish real estate companies.

[48] Gustafsson, J., & Peng, Z. (2016). Discount and Premium to NAV in Swedish Listed Property Companies (Dissertation No. 424). Retrieved from http://urn.kb.se/resolve?urn=urn:nbn:se:kth:diva-190058

Steffen, Woltering & Weis (2018)[49] ran a regression with sample of 447 real estate stocks from 12 countries, with data from 2005:01 to 2014:05. The results suggested that a decrease in the NAV, increasing the premium, would be a result of an increase company size (economics of scale), increased positive stock market and property sector sentiment and increased leverage (positive leverage effect on the return on equity). While an increase in NAV, decreasing the premium or increasing the discount (more properly said), would be of increased company specific risk and increase in the default spread.

Kjærland & Lutdal (2019)[50], as the presented research, have found similar results. They sampled 67 real estate companies from Norway, Sweden, Denmark, Finland, Germany, the Netherlands, Belgium, and the UK on annual report from 2017. The results suggested variables as size, shopping malls, commercial buildings, equity ratio and interest rate have a positive impact on the discount while diversification, earnings, interest coverage ratio, REIT status and EPRA-reporting have the opposite.

Despite these studies, the "NAV spread puzzle" still remains as a puzzle as research, and other, have stated that the variables are largely affected by the model specification. Therefore, it should not be taken for granted that an investment or real estate company, trading at a discount, is of value.

---

[49] Steffen, S., Woltering, R.O & Weis, C. (2018). New Insights into the NAV Spread Puzzle of Listed Real Estate: Idiosyncratic and Systematic Evidence. 10.15396/eres2018_224.

[50] Kjærland, F., & Lutdal, E. (2019). Do Listed Real-Estate Companies Trade at a Discount to Their Net Asset Value? Archives of Business Research, 7(8), 315-330.

Chapter 3. Discount rate

"The hardest thing to judge is what level of risk is safe."

- *George Soros*

"No matter how skillful the trading scheme, over the long haul, abnormal returns are sustained only through abnormal exposure to risk."

- *Alan Greenspan*

A severe mistake would be to choose an incorrect discount rate, which leads to a misleading estimate (risking of overpaying). Well known estimates for the discount rate are Capital Asset Pricing Model and Weighted Average Cost of Capital contingent on the cash flows. But strict assumptions and structure attenuate their capacity. The generic way to discount cash flows, (Risk-Adjusted Discount Rate Method) as have been done in previous chapter, suffers problem as the discount rate(s) is compounded, conflicting with statements et cetera. This can be resolved with Certainty Equivalent method where a different estimate for the discount rate will be presented. But prior to that, the components of Capital Asset Pricing Model and Weighted Average Cost of Capital will be presented and discussed.

3.0 The risk-free interest rate

In its essence, the discount rate (r_d) consists of a risk-free rate (r_f) and risk premium component (r_p):

$$r_d = r_f + r_p$$

Where the risk-free rate consists of a real return and an inflation premium component. The real return reflects the demanded return for forgoing current consumption (or compensation for savings), while the inflation premium compensates the investor for the loss of purchasing power. This premium varies based on the expectations, if a higher inflation were to be expected then the premium would increase and vice versa. The risk premium (the excess return over the risk-free interest rate) could be considered to be a sum of different elements such as: interest rate risk, purchasing power risk, business risk and financial risk. There are different models for how this premium should be measured. For instance, *Capital Asset Pricing Model* (CAPM) measure this as a function of the stock's systematic risk (beta), which will be presented.

Before moving to the different methods to estimate the discount rate, I would like to take some time to talk about the risk-free interest as, in most finance literature, it is implicitly assumed to be easily found. The definition, per se, of a risk-free interest rate is where its actual returns is equal to the expected. For instance, if you were expected to be paid 10 000 SEK in 6 months by a treasury bill, and it was, de facto, the payment you received (despite any adverse effect), then it could be classified as a risk-free investment (asset). However, there are two conditions that need to be fulfilled for an asset to be classified as a risk-free:

1. No default risks
2. No reinvestment risks

The first condition could be thought to be fulfilled by the government securities, not because government are better run than companies, but because they control the printing of currency (some countries) and taxation. There is situation when this is not the case, which will be returned to. The second condition is often forgotten. A government coupon bond with a maturity of 5 years, cannot be classified as a risk-free security since the coupons received are needed to be reinvested at the same price bought at (which cannot be predicted today). Therefore, it is preferable to use a zero-coupon bond as a lump sum is received at the end of the maturity.

One should match each government zero-coupon bond rate with the maturity of cash flow. For instance, if the cash flow was expected to "materialise" at the end of year 2, then it would be appropriate to use the rate from a government zero-coupon bond with a maturity of two years as the risk-free rate. But setbacks arise when zero-coupon bonds are not traded. In that case, a bootstrap methodology for the coupon bonds could be used to extract comparable zero-coupon bond rates. Assume the two following coupon bonds:

1. 1-year coupon bond, 5% coupon rate, face value of 1000, price = 950

2. 2-year coupon bond, 3% coupon rate, face value of 1000, price = 940

$$Price\ of\ 1\ year\ bond = \frac{(Face\ Value + coupon)}{(1 + r_f)} = 950 = \frac{(1000 + 50)}{(1 + r_f)} \Rightarrow r_f$$

$$= \frac{1050}{950} - 1 \approx 0.105$$

Notice the 1-year coupon bond has no reinvestment risk, as the coupon is annually and received at the end of the maturity. So, the first risk free rate for year 1 is 10.5%. This can be used for the second bond:

$$Price\ of\ 2\ year\ bond = \frac{coupon}{\left(1 + r_{f_1}\right)} + \frac{(Face\ Value + coupon)}{\left(1 + r_{f_2}\right)^2} \Rightarrow 940$$

$$= \frac{30}{(1 + 0.105)} + \frac{1030}{\left(1 + r_{f_2}\right)^2} \Rightarrow 940 - \frac{30}{(1 + 0.105)} = \frac{1030}{\left(1 + r_{f_2}\right)^2}$$

Where:

$$940 - \frac{30}{(1 + 0.105)} \approx 912.85$$

So

$$\Rightarrow \sqrt{\left(\frac{1}{912.85}\right) * 1030} - 1 = r_{f_2} \approx 0.0622$$

The problem solver in excel could also be used for these problems where $r_{f_2} \approx$ 6.22%. As for now, the risk-free rate for both year 1 and 2 are known. This methodology could get troublesome if a two-stage model were used where the first stage consisted of 15 years (15 different risk-free interest rates). A solution would be to use a risk-free interest that applies to all years. A duration matching can be used. Duration matching is the process to match the duration of its asset to its liabilities, resulting in less affection by a change in the interest rate (or even immune). The duration for cash flow for stable firms is lower than for growth firms.

To quantify, it is expected that the duration is approximately between 8 and 9 years (with the help of DDM) for a stable firm while for a growth firm it is between 20 and 25 years. The duration of a zero-coupon bond is equal to its maturity. Hence, for a stable firm, a zero-coupon bond rate with a maturity of 8 or 9 years, or a treasury bond rate with a maturity of 10 years (its duration is approximately 8 years) could be used. For a growth firm, a zero-coupon bond rate with a maturity of 20, 21, 22, 23 24, or 25 year (depending on its growth) or a treasury bond rate with a maturity of 30 years (duration close to 18 years) could be used.

The reason why the risk-free rate would differ across currencies could be because of the inflation expectations. If the inflation were expected to be higher in one currency, than the risk-free rate in that currency would be higher as a result. In some cases, there could be differences in different countries with the same currency as in the European union (excluding Denmark and Sweden). In that situation, it would be best if one took the real risk-free rate (risk-free rate subtracted with the inflation) of the country with superior structure, such as Germany, and added the expected inflation in the country of interest. A security which could be used in these situations would be an inflation-indexed treasury security as its coupon and face value are indexed against inflation where the security as a whole will report the real return.

3.1 Weighted Average Cost of Capital

The r_{wacc} stands for the *Weighted Average Cost of Capital* (WACC). Per definition, it is the cost of capital where each category of the capital is proportionately weighted. Therefore, the yield required by debt holders and stockholders are of interest. The sum of these yields should equal to the return the firm makes on its assets, since its assets consists of both equity and debts excluding for non-interest-bearing liabilities. Let us start with the net income of the firm where taxes are not presence:

$$NE = ROA * BE + (ROA - r_D) * D \Leftrightarrow NE = ROA * BE + ROA * D - Int$$

Where $ROA = \frac{EBIT}{BE+D}$ = return on the assets, $r_D = \frac{Int}{RD}$ = cost of debts and Int = interest expenses.

$$NE = ROA(BE + D) - Int \Leftrightarrow NE = ROA(BE + D) - Int = EBIT - Int$$

Since $ROE = \frac{NE}{BE}$ the equation can be expanded by dividing with BE:

$$\frac{NE}{BE} = ROA\frac{BE}{BE} + (ROA - r_D)\frac{D}{BE} = ROA + (ROA - r_D)\frac{D}{BE}$$

This relationship is called Hävstångssambandet in Swedish, as there is no good translation in English for this concept one could call this the leverage effect. This concept will be reviewed later. Before continuing, assume that t_c is presence, where $ROE^* = \frac{(EBIT-Int)(1-t_c)}{BE}$, $ROA^* = \frac{EBIT(1-t_c)}{TA}$ and the total assets (TA) consists of equity and debts solely (e.g. excluding hybrid instruments). Therefore, to adjust the equation above, multiply both LHS and RHS with $(1 - t_c)$:

$$ROE^* = ROA^* + (ROA^* - r_D[1 - t_c])\frac{D}{BE} = ROA^* + ROA^*\frac{D}{BE} - r_D(1 - t_c)\frac{D}{BE}$$

$$\Leftrightarrow$$

$$ROE^* = ROA^*\left(1 + \frac{D}{BE}\right) - r_D(1 - t_c)\frac{D}{BE}$$

Solving for ROA^*:

$$ROA^*\left(1 + \frac{D}{BE}\right) = ROE^* + r_D(1 - t_c)\frac{D}{BE}$$

$$\Rightarrow ROA^* = \frac{ROE^* + r_D(1 - t_c)\frac{D}{BE}}{1 + \frac{D}{BE}} = \frac{ROE^* + r_D(1 - t_c)\frac{D}{BE}}{\frac{BE + D}{BE}}$$

Since $\frac{BE+D}{BE} = \frac{TA}{BE}$:

$$ROA^* = \frac{ROE^* + r_D(1 - t_c)\frac{D}{BE}}{\frac{BE + D}{BE}} = \frac{ROE^* + r_D(1 - t_c)\frac{D}{BE}}{\frac{TA}{BE}}$$

$$= \frac{BE}{TA}ROE^* + \frac{D}{TA}r_D(1 - t_c)$$

The r_{wacc} is calculated as:

$$r_{wacc} = \frac{ME}{EV}r_e + \frac{MD}{EV}r_{DMD}(1-t_c)$$

Which is almost identical to ROA^* but instead of using ROE^* an estimated discount rate for the shareholders r_e is used because ROE^* can be misleading. A company could distribute a great quantity of dividends, lowering the net income for the year and indirectly, lowering ROE^*. However, r_e is not flawless due to the different assumptions required. Another distinction is to use the market value of equity and debts instead of their book value since it is more updated. In that case, r_D should be adjusted towards r_{DMD}, the market rate that the company pays on its debts. $r_{d_{MD}}$ should reflect the sum of risks associated with the company. As always, the risk-free interest rate is included but risks such as default risk (not being able to fulfils its obligations), reinvestment risk (not being able to invest its coupons to discount rate) and etc. It should be mentioned that normally debts are subtracted from cash and cash equivalents as it can lower the risk of being leveraged.

As mentioned in chapter 2, EV could also constitutes of preferences shares. Therefore, the $WACC$ could be further adjusted by:

$$r_{wacc} = \frac{ME}{EV}r_e + \frac{MD}{EV}r_{DMD}(1-t_c) + \frac{MP}{EV}r_{MP}$$

r_{MP} is the yield (payments per share divided with its price) of the preference shares while MP is the market value. This would had been reflected in ROA^* too. Lastly, minority interest could also be included. But these amendments depend on the business's stakeholders.

Personally, r_{wacc} is a greater tool to estimate the cost of capital rather than ROA^* since it is not easily affected by the decisions by the company, but it allows for subjective assumptions where cognitive biases could negatively affect the cost of capital. Further, r_{wacc} can also be misleading because of the proportion weighted. For instance, if the firm were expected to remain stable over the years, thereby using a perpetuity model, indirectly it would assume that the proportion of debts and equity remained the same over all the years which is not practice.

One situation where both ROA^* and r_{wacc} could be used would be to compare them. As the worth of a company is the sum of its investments (and operations), one could compare the ROA^* with r_{wacc} to see whether the company is able to create any excess return, $ROA^* > r_{wacc}$. The same for ROE^* and r_e as it would be preferable to invest in a stock where $ROE^* > r_e$ as this would imply that the company makes decisions where the return on equity (the aggregate of investments) would be larger than the shareholders demands. This is embedded in RIM and EVA.

Returning to the leverage effect, it was Professor Sven-Erik Johansson at Stockholm School of Economics, who launched the concept. The leverage effect is meant to perspective on the total risk defined as the variation in the expected return on equity:

$$
\begin{array}{ccccc}
\textit{Total Risk} & & \textit{Operating Risk} & & \textit{Financial Risk} \\
\downarrow & & \downarrow & & \downarrow \\
ROE & = & ROA & + & (ROA - RS)\dfrac{D}{BE}
\end{array}
$$

The operating risk measures the risk contained from the company's investment, product, price, and market policy. As the name entails, the financial risk measures the risk from financing. While the leverage effect would not help to quantify the stock price, it would aid to understand in which business the company operates in. For instance, banks expect to have high financial risk relative to the operating risk. One could plot these components as a time series to see deviation whether a company starts to move into another business area as the grocery company ICA did when it launched its bank, Ica Banken, in 2001.

Decomposing ROE differently:

$$
ROE = \frac{NI_0}{BE_0} = \frac{NI_0}{Revenue}\frac{Revenue}{TA}\frac{TA}{BE_0} = NPM * AT * EM
$$

Where $NPM = Net\ Profit\ Margin,$ $AT = Asset\ Turnover$ and $EM = Equity\ Multiplier.$

This relationship is called DuPont model. This make it easier to understand the strategies of a business. A company could increase its return on equity by increasing its profit margin, turnover or decreasing its equity according to DuPont. By increasing its profit margin, the company would either be forced to lower its cost or increasing its price on the product (high-priced strategy). The company could choose to decrease its prices rather than increase as it would increase it sales, hence the turnover would increase (low-priced strategy). Finally, by paying out dividends, ROE could increase as equity decreases. The company could also choose to increase its proportion of liabilities. The question is then whether it would provide any benefits. It is important to lay these components out in a time series to see how the company has evolved and whether the present path is correct from your perspective.

3.2 Capital Asset Pricing Model

The *Capital Asset Pricing Model* (CAPM) estimates r_e by assuming that the only risk an investor should be rewarded for, is the systematic risk since it is non-diversifiable per definition. This is measured, solely, through the beta which is equal to covariance between the stock's returns and the relevant index's returns divided with the variance of the relevant index's returns. Therefore, the model can be called as a single factor model. But before deriving CAPM, let us first derive the Capital Market Line (CML) as it is a cornerstone for CAPM. CML assumes that there is a single index market portfolio X and that investor can lend and borrow at a risk-free interest rate (r_f). Define x as the market portfolio and y as the risk-free interest asset:

$$E(R_p) = \bar{R}_p = w_x R_x + w_y R_y$$

And the variance of the portfolio:

$$\sigma_p^2 = E[R_p - \bar{R}_p]^2 = E[w_x R_x + w_y R_y - w_x \bar{R}_x - w_y \bar{R}_y]^2$$

$$= E[w_x(R_x - \bar{R}_x) + w_y(R_y - \bar{R}_y)]^2$$

By using the square rule:

$$\sigma_p^2 = E\left[w_x^2(R_x - \bar{R}_x)^2 + 2w_xw_y(R_x - \bar{R}_x)(R_y - \bar{R}_y) + w_y^2(R_y - \bar{R}_y)^2\right]$$

$$= w_x^2 E[(R_x - \bar{R}_x)^2] + 2w_xw_y E[(R_x - \bar{R}_x)(R_y - \bar{R}_y)] + w_y^2 E\left[(R_y - \bar{R}_y)^2\right]$$

$$= w_x^2\sigma_x^2 + 2w_xw_y\sigma_{x,y} + w_y^2\sigma_y^2$$

Since y is the risk-free asset the $2w_xw_y\sigma_{x,y} + w_y^2\sigma_y^2$ disappears because of its definition. Therefore:

$$\sigma_p^2 = w_x^2\sigma_x^2 \Rightarrow \frac{\sigma_p}{\sigma_x} = w_x$$

Which now can be used to describe $E(R_p)$ for the portfolio:

$$E(R_p) = w_xR_x + w_yR_y = \frac{\sigma_p}{\sigma_x}R_x + \left(1 - \frac{\sigma_p}{\sigma_x}\right)r_f = r_f + \frac{R_x - r_f}{\sigma_x}\sigma_p$$

According to CML, this describes that the only way an investor could receive a higher expected return is through an increased risk. However, it is important that one notices "expected" meaning that it is not certain that an investor would receive a higher return as a cause of an increased risk. The difference between CML and CAPM is that CML assumes there is a perfect correlation between the portfolio and stock market. CAPM assumes that the correlation is less and amend this by multiplying a correlation coefficient ($\rho_{x,y}$) to the second term:

$$E(R_p) = r_f + \frac{R_x - r_f}{\sigma_x}\sigma_p\rho_{x,y}$$

Which tells that the expected return of a portfolio is a function of the risk-free asset and risk-return trade-off $\left(\frac{R_x - r_f}{\sigma_x}\right)$ adjusted for its risk (σ_p). CAPM can be derived differently. What proportion of w_x (market portfolio) and w_y (redefining it as a risky asset) should be invested so $E(R_p)$ is maximised and σ_p^2 is minimised? Use the partial derivative of w_y:

$$E(R_p) = \bar{R}_p = w_yR_y + w_xR_x = w_yR_y + (1 - w_y)R_x$$

$$\Rightarrow \frac{\partial E(R_p)}{\partial w_y} = R_y - R_x$$

$$\sigma_p^2 = w_y^2 \sigma_y^2 + 2w_x w_y \sigma_{x,y} + w_x^2 \sigma_x^2 = w_y^2 \sigma_y^2 + 2w_y(1 - w_y)\sigma_{x,y} + (1 - w_y)^2 \sigma_y^2$$

$$\Rightarrow \frac{\partial \sigma_p^2}{\partial w_y} = \frac{2w_y \sigma_y^2 - 2(1 - w_y)\sigma_x^2 + 2(1 - 2w_y)\sigma_{y,x}}{2\sqrt{2w_y \sigma_y^2 + 2(1 - w_y)^2 \sigma_x^2 + 2w_y(1 - w_y)\sigma_{y,x}}}$$

As CAPM assumes that all investors use identical analysis of the same universe of assets, the market portfolio already includes the risky asset. So, w_y mirrors an excess demand for the risky asset. But no general equilibrium will exist. Therefore, rewrite the partial derivatives, given that $w_y = 0$, as:

$$\frac{\partial E(R_p)}{\partial w_y} = R_y - R_x$$

$$\frac{\partial \sigma_p}{\partial w_y} = \frac{\sigma_{y,x} - \sigma_x^2}{\sigma_x}$$

Divide these equations with each other as it is wondered what the risk-return trade-off would be:

$$\frac{\dfrac{\partial E(R_p)}{\partial w_y}}{\dfrac{\partial \sigma_p}{\partial w_y}} = \frac{R_y - R_x}{\dfrac{\sigma_{y,x} - \sigma_x^2}{\sigma_x}} = \frac{R_y - R_x}{\sigma_{y,x} - \sigma_x^2}\sigma_x$$

Where it is known from CML that:

$$E(R_p) = r_f + \frac{R_x - r_f}{\sigma_x}\sigma_p$$

$\frac{R_x - r_f}{\sigma_x}$ represents the risk-return trade-off. Therefore, to arrive to CAPM equalise the risk-return trade-off above with CML's

$$\frac{R_y - R_x}{\sigma_{y,x} - \sigma_x^2}\sigma_x = \frac{R_x - r_f}{\sigma_x}$$

Solving for R_y gives:

$$\frac{R_y - R_x}{\sigma_{y,x} - \sigma_x^2}\sigma_x = \frac{R_x - r_f}{\sigma_x} \Rightarrow (R_y - R_x)\sigma_x = \frac{R_x - r_f}{\sigma_x}(\sigma_{y,x} - \sigma_x^2)$$

$$\Rightarrow \frac{R_x(\sigma_{y,x} - \sigma_x^2) - r_f(\sigma_{y,x} - \sigma_x^2)}{\sigma_x}$$

$$\Rightarrow \frac{R_x(\sigma_{y,x} - \sigma_x^2)}{\sigma_x} - \frac{r_f(\sigma_{y,x} - \sigma_x^2)}{\sigma_x} \Rightarrow \frac{R_x \sigma_{y,x}}{\sigma_x} - R_x \sigma_x - \frac{r_f \sigma_{y,x}}{\sigma_x} + r_f \sigma_x$$

So:

$$(R_y - R_x) = \frac{R_x \sigma_{y,x}}{\sigma_x^2} - R_x - \frac{r_f \sigma_{y,x}}{\sigma_x^2} + r_f$$

$$R_y = \frac{R_x \sigma_{y,x}}{\sigma_x^2} - \frac{r_f \sigma_{y,x}}{\sigma_x^2} + r_f \Rightarrow \frac{R_x \sigma_{y,x} - r_f \sigma_{y,x}}{\sigma_x^2} + r_f \Rightarrow \frac{R_x - r_f}{\sigma_x^2}\sigma_{y,x} + r_f$$

$$\Rightarrow r_f + \frac{\sigma_{y,x}}{\sigma_x^2}(R_x - r_f)$$

Where $\beta = \frac{\sigma_{y,x}}{\sigma_x^2}$, hence:

$$R_y = r_f + \beta(R_x - r_f)$$

Here it can be seen that the expected return of a risky asset is a function of the risk-free interest and compensated risk premium $(R_x - r_f)$ adjusting for the stock's market risk (β).

What should be the expected return of a stock when the risk-free interest is 2%, beta of the stock 1.5, and the expected market return 7%:

$$r_e = r_f + \beta(R_x - r_f) = 0.02 + 1.5(0.07 - 0.02) = 0.095 = 9.5\%$$

A common mistake is to think that a beta of 2 means that the expected return of a stock would be doubled than its market. This is not the case, conditioned on $r_f > 0$:

$$r_e = r_f + \beta(R_x - r_f) \Rightarrow r_f + 2(R_x - r_f) = r_f + 2R_x - 2r_f = 2R_x - r_f$$

While CAPM is simple to estimate r_e, its assumptions seem unrealistic as its assumptions are:

1. The expected return and standard deviation are the only two things investors care about

2. Two assets are correlated because of their correlation with the market

3. The returns over a single period are what investors focus on, which are the same across all investors

4. Investors can borrow and lend at the risk-free interest rate

5. Taxes do not influence the investors' decisions

6. Investors' estimates of the expected returns, standard deviations and correlations are homogenous

3.3 Unlevered beta

It is preferable to decompose the beta into an unleveraged component (*Unlevered beta*) to get a better sense of how the beta would change if the company decided to increase its debts. Further, by decomposing and using an average of other related companies unlevered beta for a specific company, outliners would be a less severe problem. The unlevered beta is calculated as:

$$\beta_u = \frac{\beta_L}{1 + \frac{D}{E}(1 - t_c)}$$

To derive, denote the market value of an unlevered firm as EV_u and the market value of equity as E_u for an unlevered firm. As the firm is unlevered, has no debts, the market value of the firm should be equal to the equity, where it can be assumed that there are no cash and cash equivalents as it would not provide with any hindsight for the derivation. Further denote the market value of a firm as EV_L and the market value of equity as E_L and market value of debts as D_L for a levered firm. The difference between the unlevered and levered firm is the debts provides a tax shield (see the Appendix for *Adjusted Present Value* [APV]) as the interest expenses from the debts lower the taxes contingent on $t_c > 0$. The (interest) tax shield (*ITS*) can be written as:

$$ITS_t = r_D D_{L,t} t_c$$

Where the present value of ITS is:

$$PV(ITS_t) = \sum_{t}^{n} \frac{r_D D_{L,t} t_c}{(1 + r_D)^t} = V$$

So far, it is known that $EV_u = E_u$ and $EV_L = E_L + D_L$. But EV_L can be written as $E_u + V$ according to APV. Equate these two equations and solve for E_L:

$$E_L + D_L = E_u + V \Rightarrow E_L = E_u + V - D_L$$

The beta of a portfolio (B_p) is the weighted average of its components' betas:

$$V_p = V_1 + V_2 + V_3$$

Where B_p is:

$$B_p = \left(\frac{V_1}{V_p}\right)\beta_1 + \left(\frac{V_2}{V_p}\right)\beta_2 + \left(\frac{V_3}{V_p}\right)\beta_3$$

Apply this to E_L:

$$\beta_{E_L} = \left(\frac{E_u}{E_L}\right)\beta_{E_u} + \left(\frac{V}{E_L}\right)\beta_V - \left(\frac{D_L}{E_L}\right)\beta_{D_L} = \left(1 + \frac{D_L - V}{E_L}\right)\beta_{E_u} + \left(\frac{V}{E_L}\right)\beta_V - \left(\frac{D_L}{E_L}\right)\beta_{D_L}$$

Before the conclusion is reached, three assumptions are needed. The first is that the company holds a constant dollar amount of debt (one of the assumptions made by APV). This leads to:

$$PV(ITS_t) = \sum_{t}^{n} \frac{r_D D_{L,t} t_c}{(1 + r_D)^t} = \frac{r_D D_{L,t} t_c}{r_D} = D_L t_c$$

The second one is that $\beta_V = \beta_{D_L}$:

$$\beta_{E_L} = \left(1 + \frac{D_L - D_L t_c}{E_L}\right)\beta_{E_u} + \left(\frac{D_L t_c}{E_L}\right)\beta_{D_L} - \left(\frac{D_L}{E_L}\right)\beta_{D_L}$$

$$= \left(1 + \frac{(1 - t_c)D_L}{E_L}\right)\beta_{E_u} + \left(\frac{D_L t_c}{E_L}\right)\beta_{D_L} - \left(\frac{D_L}{E_L}\right)\beta_{D_L}$$

And the third $\beta_{D_L} = 0$. Now the beta of a stock can be decomposed into a levered component and unlevered component:

$$\beta_L = \beta_U \left(1 + \frac{(1 - t_c)D_L}{E_L}\right) \Rightarrow \beta_U = \frac{\beta_L}{1 + \frac{(1 - t_c)D_L}{E_L}}$$

It is preferable to decompose similar stocks' unlevered beta and compute a weighted average of unlevered betas to use it for a specific stock:

$$\left(1 + \frac{(1 - t_c)D_L}{E_L}\right)\frac{1}{n}\sum_t^n \beta_{U_t} = \beta_L$$

Assume the following information about stock A, with current stock price of 29 SEK:

Per Share	2019 (0)	2020 (1)	2021 (2)	2022 (3)
Div_t		5	5.25	5.355
g			0.05	0.02
Debts	850			
Equity	1200			
t_c	0.4			
B_L	1.4			

But before discounting the dividends, r_e needs to be estimated with can be done by CAPM. However, it is unsure whether the beta for stock A is accurate. Therefore, it would be preferable, in this example, to use similar stocks' beta. Assume following for stock B - E with similar characteristics as stock A:

β_U for B	0.9
β_U for C	0.8
β_U for D	0.95
β_U for E	0.7
Average	0.8375

By plugging the numbers in the formula for β_L:

$$\beta_L = \left(1 + \frac{(1-t_c)D_L}{E_L}\right)\frac{1}{n}\sum_t^n \beta_{U_t} = \left(1 + \frac{(1-0.4)850}{1200}\right)\frac{0.9 + 0.8 + 0.95 + 0.7}{4}$$

$$= 1.19$$

With a risk-free interest of 1% and risk premium of 7%:

$$r_e = 0.01 + 1.19 * 0.07 = 0.0933 = 9.33\%$$

It is expected that the stock A, after year 2, will stabilise its financials, resulting in a discount rate at 7%, hence a two-stage model should be used:

Per Share	2019 (0)	2020 (1)	2021 (2)	2022 (3)
Div_t		5	5.25	5.355
g			0.05	0.02
r_e		0.0933	0.0933	0.07
$\sum_{t=1}^T \frac{Div_t}{(1+r_e)^t}$		4.57	4.39	
$\frac{Div_{T+1}}{r_{e_{T+1}}(1+r_e)^T}$			89.60	
P_0	98.57			

It should be mentioned that some would prefer to define D_L as the market value of debts after cash (by subtracting) if the cash and cash equivalents are of significant proportion, as for WACC. Why cash and cash equivalents was not included as component in EV is because cash is normally assumed to have a beta of 0. Therefore, it is more common to subtract the debts from the cash and cash equivalents.

3.4 Arbitrage Pricing Theory (APT)

According to PriceWaterhouseCoopers's (PwC) risk premium report in 2019, 91% of the respondents, working in represented finance departments, said that a size premium is added in addition to CAPM. The size of a company matters as small cap tends to have a greater volatility than large cap, making investors demanding a greater premium for small cap, ceteris paribus. In USA, Duff & Phelps "Cost of Capital Navigator" is the main source for the size premium which is yearly updated. In Sweden, one could use PWC report, issued once per year in May, where PWC asks the responders to quantity the size premium into four different classes. Duff & Phelps estimation is similar to *Arbitrage Pricing Theory* (APT). Unlike CAPM, APT assumes that sometimes misprice of securities occur before the market corrects. Therefore, the APT extends the CAPM with additional macroeconomics factors. Further, APT assumes that investors do not hold efficient portfolios as CAPM assumes. But APT has three underlying assumptions:

1. The return of a stock is explained by its systematic factors
2. The specific risk can be eliminated through diversification
3. Arbitrage opportunity does not exist among well-diversified portfolios as the specific risk is eliminated in 2. If this was the case, then it would be exploited away by the market participants.

The factors in APT are unidentified, which makes the model an "open-source". Hence, the model could be extended to n factors:

$$R_i = r_f + \beta_1^i \Phi_1 + \beta_2^i \Phi_2 + \cdots + \beta_n^i \Phi_n$$

Where:

$$\Phi_i = r_{i\,of\,interest} - r_f$$

For each stock (or probably each branch) the APT could be different. This is a severe disadvantage of APT as it is time consuming. However, a well-known specification of APT model is Fama and French Three Factor Model. They stated that that the expected return of an asset R_i, can be computed as:

$$R_i = r_f + \beta^i_{market} E(r_{market} - r_f) + \beta^i_{SMB} E(SMB) + \beta^i_{HML} E(HML)$$

Where SMB (small minus big) and HML (high minus low) are the expected return of size factor and the book-to-market equity factor. The SMB regards the excess return of small cap stocks compared to the market while HML regards stocks with high book-to-market ratios that have excess returns compared to the market. The betas for these can be estimated by running time series regressions on historical data as the beta will be computed differently when we have more than one coefficient (β_i).

3.5 Manipulating the model discount rate

One could derive the implied discount rate. Recall the non-growing perpetuity model for RIM:

$$P_0 = \frac{NI_1}{r_e}$$

Solving for r_e:

$$P_0 = \frac{NI_1}{r_e} \Rightarrow \frac{P_0}{NI_1} = \frac{1}{r_e} \Rightarrow r_e = \frac{1}{\frac{P_0}{NI_1}} = \frac{NI_1}{P_0}$$

The $\frac{P_0}{NI_1}$ is called the forward price to earnings as it calculated what the ratio between them too should be based on the stock price today and the expected net income in year 1. By rewriting models, used to quantify the stock price, one could get an estimate of what discount rate is according to the market participants (hence the name "implied"). This method is called the Internal Rate of Return (IRR, or yield to maturity for fixed income securities). It gets difficulty if "correct" model is assumed to be a two-stage. However, this will be discussed in chapter 4 for IRR.

3.6 Certainty Equivalent Method

There are some disadvantages described so far. As for CAPM, it assumes that the capital market is complete and perfect which is not accurate in practice. A second problem, including the risk premium in the discount rate makes the risk premium compounding over time, implying the farther into the future, the riskier the cash flows. One may argue that the future brings uncertainty but recall the assumption about the terminal value where the company is supposed to be stable, implying less risk. The third problem is if the cash flows are negative for one year. It might not be the case for dividends, but if the free cash flows of equity are of interest the problem could arise. Since discounting negative cash flows would increase their present value, implying that negative cash flows are preferred now rather than delaying and receiving lesser later. One method that tackle these issues is the *Certainty Equivalent* (CE) method. The methods described earlier are classified as *Risk-Adjusted Discount Rate* (RADR) method. The CE follows the concept of utility theory where one needs to analyse the cash flow's risk and later specify how much of these cash flows are, with certainty, are expected to be retrieved. To illustrate CE, assume the cash flow in year 1 is of interest, where the discount rate is $= r_f + r_p$:

$$PV(CF_1) = \frac{E(CF_1)}{1 + r_f + r_p} \Rightarrow PV(CF_1)(1 + r_f + r_p) = E(CF_1)$$

$$\Rightarrow PV(CF_1)r_p + PV(CF_1)(1 + r_f)$$

$$= E(CF_1) \Rightarrow PV(CF_1) = \frac{E(CF_1) - PV(CF_1)r_p}{(1 + r_f)} = \frac{CEQ_0[CF_1]}{(1 + r_f)}$$

The CEQ_0 is called the certainty equivalent value where its value is the expected cash flow in year 1 subtracted with the reduction caused by the risk. The risk associated with the cash flows in year 1 is needed to be analysed. There are different methods for this but Zhang (2010)[51] proposed a method that is logical and consistent in its approach. Zhang states that a put option can be used to retrieve the coefficient for the risk. Denote the expected cash flow as X, d as the certainty equivalent coefficient and the CEQ as Xd.

Risk equivalent $= X - Xd$

---

[51] Zhang, Z. Certainty equivalent, risk premium and asset pricing. Front. Bus. Res. China 4, 325–339 (2010). https://doi.org/10.1007/s11782-010-0015-1

Where:

$$Xd = X - Risk\ equivalent$$

A certain cash flow is expected where its risk is being below than the expected value.

To eliminate this risk, a "guarantee" is needed. This is solved with the put option as it gives the owner the right (not the obligation) to sell a specific amount of the underlying security (cash flow as in this example). So, the risk equivalent can be retrieved by calculating the value of a put, where Black Scholes pricing model is used as it is the most convenient model used to value standard European put option (P):

$$P = Xe^{-r_f t}N(-d_2) - SN(-d_1)$$

Where t is the maturity time, X is the strike price or, in this case, the expected cash flow at the maturity date and S is the current value of the expected cash flow. Notice the assumption about continuous compounded returns ($e^{-r_f T}$). While it out of the scope to mathematically show this relationship holds, I would refer to the book "Options, Futures, and Other Derivatives, Global Edition" by John C. Hull for the derivation of Black Scholes. $N(-d_1)$ and $N(-d_2)$ are the cumulative probability under standard normal distribution of the variables $-d_1$ and $-d_2$ where:

$$d_1 = \frac{\ln\left(\frac{S}{Xe^{-r_f t}}\right)}{\sigma\sqrt{t}} + \frac{\sigma\sqrt{t}}{2}$$

And

$$d_2 = \frac{\ln\left(\frac{S}{Xe^{-r_f t}}\right)}{\sigma\sqrt{t}} - \frac{\sigma\sqrt{t}}{2} = d_1 - \sigma\sqrt{t}$$

Where σ is the annual standard deviation of the change between the forecasted values. According to Andrew, Turner, and Weigel (1992)[52] the σ ranges between 20% to 60% for stock prices where safer stocks would be approximately closer to 20% and riskier would be closer to 60%. Zhang argues that, as cash flows are generic less volatile than the stock price, the forecasted values (cash flows) should be in a range of 10% to 40%.

Recall that the S is the present value of the cash flow (X), so the value of the put option can be rewritten as:

$$P = Xe^{-r_f t}N(-d_2) - SN(-d_1) = Xe^{-r_f t}[N(-d_2) - N(-d_1)]$$

$$= Xe^{-r_f t}\left[N\left(\sigma\sqrt{t/4}\right) - N\left(-\sigma\sqrt{t/4}\right)\right]$$

$$= Xe^{-r_f t}\left\{N\left(\sigma\sqrt{t/4}\right) - \left[1 - N\left(\sigma\sqrt{t/4}\right)\right]\right\}$$

Or:

$$P = Xe^{-r_f t}\left[2N\left(\sigma\sqrt{t/4}\right) - 1\right]$$

As the future value is of interest, multiply the equation above with $e^{r_f t}$ to retrieve the risk equivalent:

$$Risk\ equivalent = Xe^{-r_f t}\left[2N\left(\sigma\sqrt{t/4}\right) - 1\right]e^{r_f T} = X\left[2N\left(\sigma\sqrt{t/4}\right) - 1\right]$$

Which means:

$$Xd = X - Risk\ equivalent = X - X\left[2N\left(\sigma\sqrt{t/4}\right) - 1\right] = 2X\left[1 - N\left(\sigma\sqrt{t/4}\right)\right]$$

Where d can be separated as:

$$2\left[1 - N\left(\sigma\sqrt{t/4}\right)\right]$$

---

[52] Turner, A., & Weigel, E. (1992). Daily Stock Market Volatility: 1928-1989. Management Science, 38(11), 1586-1609.

One could use excel to retrieve this formula: 2*(1-NORM.S.DIST($\sigma\sqrt{t/4}$, TRUE). As an example, assume that the volatility is 30% and forecast of cash flows is till year 5, then the CEQ is (per share):

Year	1	2	3	4	5
CF in SEK	25	30	45	30	40
d	0.88	0.83	0.8	0.76	0.74
CEQ in SEK	22.02	24.96	35.78	45.85	29.49

With a risk-free interest of 4%, the present value of these cash flows would be:

$$PV(CF) = \sum_{t=1}^{n} \frac{CEQ_t}{e^{r_f t}} = \frac{22.02}{e^{0.04*1}} + \frac{24.96}{e^{0.04*2}} + \frac{35.78}{e^{0.04*3}} + \frac{45.85}{e^{0.04*4}} + \frac{29.49}{e^{0.04*5}} = 139.49 \; SEK$$

The discount factor is $e^{r_f t}$ since d is derived from a model (BSM) that assumes continuous compounding returns.

It can be seen that d decreases with time, therefore as $\sigma\sqrt{t/4}$ approaches ∞ the $N\left(\sigma\sqrt{t/4}\right)$ will become 1, making $d = 0$ and $CEQ_\infty = 0$. If $T = 0$, then $d = 1$. This relationship describes that the coefficient reaches a maximum of 1 (when the cash flows are certain) and approach 0 at an infinity number of years. The models, in chapter 1, do not hold for this method of discounting regarding the terminal value as d is dynamic so $\sum_{t=1}^{n} \frac{CEQ_t}{e^{r_f t}}$ can only be used. If a perpetuity model were used with RADR, the quantified stock price would be underestimated as RADR simultaneously adjust for time and risk (compounding) while CE separates between them two.

The equation for d could be used to adjust how the discount rate should be calculated to account for both the systematic and non-systematic risk. d reflect the riskiness with cash flow at time t, which should be equal to the continuous compounded risk premium:

$$d = 2\left[1 - N\left(\sigma\sqrt{t/4}\right)\right] = e^{-r_p t}$$

Where r_p is the annual risk premium:

$$d = 2\left[1 - N\left(\sigma\sqrt{t/4}\right)\right] = e^{-r_p t} \Rightarrow \ln\left\{2\left[1 - N\left(\sigma\sqrt{t/4}\right)\right]\right\} = -r_p t$$

$$\Rightarrow r_p = -\frac{\ln\left\{2\left[1 - N\left(\sigma\sqrt{t/4}\right)\right]\right\}}{t}$$

Recall in the beginning of this chapter that $r_d = r_f + r_p$ which can now be written as:

$$r_d = r_f + r_p = r_f - \frac{\ln\left\{2\left[1 - N\left(\sigma\sqrt{t/4}\right)\right]\right\}}{t}$$

This method should be preferred as it accounts for the non-systematic risk which CAPM does not as it assumes that the investor holds a perfect diversification among its securities. Furthermore, this adjustment of method displays one important principle, that the longer the holding period, the lower the risk as temporally shocks are alleviated (or eliminated). While CAPM assumes that the decrease in total risk (to the systematic risk) is because of the perfect diversification, eliminating the firm specific risk, this amendment of the discount rate accounts for the diversification among the holding periods. This adjustment will make the discount rate identical to the CE approach. Let us return to the previous example:

Year	1	2	3	4	5
CF in SEK	25	30	45	30	40
d	0.88	0.83	0.8	0.76	0.74

Where the risk-free interest was 4%, and $\sigma = 30\%$. Further assume the cash flows are discounted with a continuous compounding rate, where the present value I uses the CE model and present value II uses RADR:

Year	1	2	3	4	5
CF in SEK	25	30	45	30	40
d	0.88	0.83	0.8	0.76	0.74
CEQ	22.02	24.96	35.78	45.85	29.49
$e^{-r_f T}$	0.96	0.92	0.89	0.85	0.82
Present Value I	21.16	23.04	31.73	39.07	24.15
r_d	0.17	0.13	0.12	0.11	0.10
$e^{-r_d T}$	0.85	0.77	0.71	0.65	0.60
Present Value II	21.16	23.04	31.73	39.07	24.15

As can be seen, adjustment by accounting the total risk in the discount rate (both the systematic and non-systematic) and the holing period effect, results in a present value of cash flows identical to the CE method. Further notice that this relationship only holds if discount factor is continuously compounded. This can mathematically be seen, at year 1:

$$\frac{CEQ_1}{e^{r_f}} = \frac{CF_1 * d}{e^{r_f}} = \frac{CF_1 * e^{-r_p}}{e^{r_f}} = \frac{CF_1}{e^{r_f + r_p}}$$

But what if the cash flows are not continuous compounded? Then the equation above would not hold. However, at year t, at an annually compounded discount rate, the relationship between CE and RADR can be specified as:

$$\frac{CF_t}{(1 + r_d)^t} = \frac{CF_t * d_t}{(1 + r_f)^t}$$

Where solving for d_t:

$$\frac{CF_t}{(1 + r_d)^t} = \frac{CF_t * d_t}{(1 + r_f)^t} \Rightarrow \frac{(1 + r_f)^t CF_t}{(1 + r_d)^t CF_t} = d_t = \frac{(1 + r_f)^t}{(1 + r_d)^t}$$

Recall:

$$r_d = r_f + r_p$$

Where:

$$r_p = -\frac{\ln\left\{2\left[1 - N\left(\sigma\sqrt{t/4}\right)\right]\right\}}{t}$$

Hence:

$$r_d = r_f - \frac{\ln\left\{2\left[1 - N\left(\sigma\sqrt{t/4}\right)\right]\right\}}{t}$$

So:

$$d_t = \frac{\left(1 + r_f\right)^t}{\left(1 + r_f - \frac{\ln\left\{2\left[1 - N\left(\sigma\sqrt{t/4}\right)\right]\right\}}{t}\right)^t}$$

Implementing this relationship in the table will make the annual RADR equal to CE method. One could also go the other way around, by asking what the r_d should be given that d_t is known:

$$\frac{CF_t}{(1 + r_a)^t} = \frac{CF_t * d_t}{(1 + r_f)^t} \Rightarrow CF_t = \frac{CF_t * d_t}{(1 + r_f)^t}(1 + r_a)^t \Rightarrow \frac{CF_t(1 + r_f)^t}{CF_t * d_t} = (1 + r_a)^t$$

$$\Rightarrow \frac{1 + r_f}{\sqrt{d_t}} - 1 = r_a$$

Further, if it was thought that the discount rate was to be compounded at a different rate than annually or continuously, for instance at a rate of i, then solving for d_t:

$$\frac{\frac{CF_t}{i}}{\left(1 + \frac{r_a}{i}\right)^{it}} = \frac{\frac{CF_t}{i} * d_t}{\left(1 + \frac{r_f}{i}\right)^{it}} \Rightarrow \frac{\left(1 + \frac{r_f}{i}\right)^{it}}{\left(1 + \frac{r_a}{i}\right)^{it}} = d_t$$

One could wonder whether the discount rate reflects the discount rate for shareholders or for both the shareholders and lenders. Well, it depends on the cash flows of interest, since these were FCFF in the example, the discount rate would be a reflection of the whole firm (as the standard deviation of cash flows are calculated), vice versa. If the cash flows were to reflect the shareholders, such as FCFE, dividends, RIM etc than it could be said that the standard deviation in BSM for estimating d could be the standard deviation of the stock's returns with the argument that the stock returns is an embedded reflection of the expected cash flow from a company. But recall Zhang argument that the standard deviation of cash flows is usually lower than the returns. It is of importance to choose the correct cash flows, for both the discount and valuing, for instance it would not be of interest by using the FCFE for a bank as it is in generic volatile relative to its stock price.

While there has been evidence that earnings are not well correlated with the stock price, it has been suggested that the stock market evaluates management's decisions based on the expected long-term cash flow impact. As Copeland (1996)[53] stated that the value of a business is the discounted expected cash flows at a discount rate that reflects the risk, it could be concluded that the stock price, itself, is a good indication of the long-term cash flows and the volatility of the stock price is a good measure for the risk related to the cash flows.

While limitations such as a perpetuity model cannot be used, CE is still seen as the superior choice compared to RADR[54]. As mentioned, RADR do not separate time and risk while CE do, creating a difference which will depend on the number of periods (years, quarter, etc) the cash flow is from the present. However, it could be converged so that RADR agrees with CE, which would give an accurate discount rate.

---

[53] Copeland, Tom; Tim Koller, and Jack Murrin, Valuation: Measuring and Managing the Value of Companies, 2nd edition, John Wiley & Sons (1996).

[54] Gitman, Lawrence J., C. Zutter. (2015). Principles of Managerial Finance, 13th edition, HarperCollins.

Sick, G. A. (1986). A certainty-equivalent approach to capital budgeting. Financial Management, Winter, 23-32.

Ben-Tal, a, and M, Teboulle. (2007). An old-new concept of convex risk measures: The optimized certainty equivalent, Mathematical Finance 17(3), 449-476

Megginson, W. L., (1997). Corporate Finance Theory, Addison-Wesley, 277-281.

3.7 Summary

It is difficult to say which discount rate one should use as there are various approaches. While CAPM is easy to use, APT is exigent but more explainable in relation to the variation of discount rate(s). But both suffer the build-up effects which can be mitigated by using the CE method. However, one could prefer to add more risk to avoid an underestimation of the discount rate.

Questions for chapter 3

1. If stock A has a debt to equity of 35%, cost of equity of 7%, cost of debt of 3% and a tax rate of 30%, what is the WACC?

2. If stock B has an equity to debt of 45%, unlevered beta of 0.7, cost of debt of 3% and a tax rate of 30% where the expected risk premium is 8% and expected return of the market 10%, what is the WACC?

3. Assume the following information for stock C:

Stock C	
Debts	650 MSEK
Equity	1000 MSEK
t_c	0.3

And further:

Unlevered beta for	
β_U for B	0.9
β_U for D	0.8
β_U for E	0.95
β_U for F	0.7

With a risk-free interest rate of 4% and expected return by the market of 11%, what is the discount rate for the shareholders, measured through CAPM?

4. As stock D is traded at 15 SEK with an expected dividend per share of 2 SEK and a growth equal to the GDP's growth, 2%, what is the implied discount rate conditioned that the firm is expected to remain stable?

5. Assume the certainty equivalent coefficient (d) to be 0.78 for stock E in year 1 with an expected risk-free interest rate of 3%, what would the:

    i.   Annual risk premium be

    ii.   Quarterly risk premium be

    iii.   Monthly risk premium be

3.8 Appendix

3.8.1 Adjusted Present Value

WACC could be used to decompose a perpetuity model (or a two-stage) of FCFF into an unlevered part and levered. This model is called Adjusted Present Value (APV). APV is defined as the present value of cash flows if the company where solely financed by equity and the present value of financing benefits. Given a perpetuity model of FCFF, EV could be defined as (through APV):

$$EV = \frac{FCFF}{r_u} + \frac{MDt_c r_D}{r_u} = APV$$

Where r_u is:

$$r_u = \frac{ME}{EV} r_e + \frac{MD}{EV} r_{DMD}$$

As for the derivation of APV, it is known that:

$$r_{wacc} = \frac{ME}{EV} r_e + \frac{MD}{EV} r_{DMD}(1 - t_c) = \frac{ME}{EV} r_e + \frac{MD}{EV} r_{DMD} - \frac{MD}{EV} r_{DMD} t_c$$

$\frac{MD}{EV} r_{DMD} t_c$ is the part that can be seen as the benefit of being leverage as interest expenses lowers the taxes. Multiply RHS and LHS with EV:

$$EV r_{wacc} = ME r_e + MD r_{DMD} - MD r_{DMD} t_c$$

Since LHS is equal to $FCFF$ $\left(EV = \frac{FCFF}{r_{wacc}} \Rightarrow EV r_{wacc} = FCFF \right)$:

$$FCFF = ME r_e + MD r_{DMD} - MD r_{DMD} t_c$$

Continue by dividing RHS and LHS by EV:

$$\frac{FCFF}{EV} = \frac{ME}{EV} r_e + \frac{MD}{EV} r_{DMD} - \frac{MD}{EV} r_{DMD} t_c$$

As $r_u = \frac{ME}{EV} r_e + \frac{MD}{EV} r_{dMD}$:

$$\frac{FCFF}{EV} = r_u - \frac{MD}{EV} r_{DMD} t_c$$

Multiply RHS and LHS by EV and divide with r_u:

$$FCFF = r_u EV - MDr_{D_{MD}}t_c \Rightarrow EV = \frac{FCFF}{r_u} + \frac{MDr_{D_{MD}}t_c}{r_u}$$

APV is used to understand the benefits of leverage $\left(EV - \frac{FCFF}{r_u} = \frac{MDr_{D_{MD}}t_c}{r_u} = \right.$ $benefits\left.\right)$ while it also can be used to estimate the value of firm.

3.9.2 Systematic risk & Firm specific risk

One important subject to mention is the difference between the *systematic risk* and *firm specific risk*. Risk itself can be decompose to a systematic and firm specific part. The systematic risk is referred to the risk that you cannot diversify. For an instance, under the financial crisis in 2008 and Covid-19 in 2020, there was a great probability that one's investments would also have declined unproportionally to the stock market. As for the firm specific risk, it can be reduced or eliminated by diversifying since the risk is associated with the company itself. If a stock announces profit warning, the shareholder would be less affected if the portfolio consisted of 40 different stocks as more movements are integrated. CAPM can be used to illustrate this. Assume that:

$$r_i = r_f + \beta_i(r_{market} - r_f) + \varepsilon_i \Rightarrow \varepsilon_i = r_i - r_f - \beta_i(r_{market} - r_f)$$

Where ε_i is the error term. This is included as it is expected that CAPM would not be precise to estimate r_i. It is further assumed that $E[\varepsilon_i] = 0$. Before proceeding, calculate the covariance of ε_i and r_{market}:

$$cov(r_i, \varepsilon_i) = cov[r_i - r_f - \beta_i(r_{market} - r_f), r_{market}]$$
$$= cov[r_i - \beta_i(r_{market} - r_f), r_{market}]$$
$$= cov(r_i, r_{market}) - \beta_i cov(r_{market} - r_f, r_{market})$$
$$= cov(r_i, r_{market}) - \beta_i cov(r_{market}, r_{market})$$
$$= \sigma_{i,market} - \frac{\sigma_{i,market}}{\sigma^2_{market}}\sigma^2_{market} = \sigma_{i,market} - \sigma_{i,market} = 0$$

Notice that the covariance between the stock market and risk-free interest is 0 but also that β_i is a constant. This tells that the error term is uncorrelated with the market, and since $E[\varepsilon_i] = 0$, the variance of r_i is:

$$var(r_i) = var(r_f) + var[\beta_i(r_{market} - r_f)] + var(\varepsilon_i) = \beta_i^2 \sigma_{market}^2 + \sigma_{\varepsilon_i}^2$$

The systematic risk refers to the risk associated with the stock market, hence it can be concluded that $\beta_i^2 \sigma_{market}^2$ is the systematic risk as it contains β_i and $\sigma_{\varepsilon_i}^2$ is the firm specific risk. By including more stock, $\sigma_{\varepsilon_i}^2$ will be reduced, possibly be eliminated as the number of stocks increases in portfolio. This can be illustrated by the usage of a single index model. "Modern Portfolio Theory and Investment Analysis" by Edwin J. Elton is recommended for further information.

3.9.3 Tobin's q
Ben-Horim and Callen laid out some interesting work in the summer of 1989[55]. First, Tobin's q could be used as an alternative measure for the discount rate. Secondly, it could also be used to measure the duration (Macaulay, returning back to in chapter 4). In its essence, Tobin's q is usually used to measure industry concentration. Its calculation it the ratio between the market value of assets (for a company) and its replacement value. As it is not clear what the replacement value would be, Ben-Horim and Callen propose a solution. They stated that the market value of a firm can be calculated as (with no debt):

$$MV = RC + F + M$$

Where RC is the replacement cost of the firm's assets, F is the capitalized value of rents attributable to firm-specific factors and M is the capitalized value of rents attributable to monopoly profits. This relationship could be estimated through a constant growth model (growing perpetuity) where:

[55] Ben-Horim, M. and Callen, J.L. (1989), THE COST OF CAPITAL, MACAULAY'S DURATION, AND TOBIN'S q . Journal of Financial Research, 12: 143-156. doi:10.1111/j.1475-6803.1989.tb00109.x

$$MV = \frac{(1-c)NI_1}{r_e - cRoe} = \frac{NI_1}{Roe} + \frac{(Roe - r_e)NI_1}{Roe(r_e - cRoe)}$$

The Roe is the expected return on equity and c is company's investment rate which is equal to the expected value of retention rate plus the expected stock financing rate. The equation above is just a growing perpetuity dividend model as it can be expressed:

$$\frac{(1-c)NI_1}{r_e - cRoe} = \frac{(1-b)NI_1}{r_e - bRoe}$$

So, $\frac{NI_1}{Roe} = RC = BE_1$ and $\frac{(Roe-r_e)NI_1}{Roe(r_e-cRoe)} = F + M$. Recall that the Tobin's q is the market value of assets divided by the replacement cost, which means that:

$$q = \frac{MV}{RC} = \frac{\frac{NI_1}{Roe} + \frac{(Roe - r_e)NI_1}{Roe(r_e - cRoe)}}{\frac{NI_1}{Roe}} = \frac{Roe - cRoe}{r_e - cRoe} = \frac{Roe(1-c)}{r_e - cRoe}$$

Now r_e can be expressed as a function of q:

$$q = \frac{Roe(1-c)}{r_e - cRoe} \Rightarrow r_e - cRoe = \frac{Roe(1-c)}{q} \Rightarrow r_e = \frac{Roe(1-c)}{q} + cRoe$$

Since:

$$q = \frac{MV}{RC} = \frac{MV}{\frac{NI_1}{Roe}} = Roe\frac{MV}{NI_1}$$

And:

$$q = Roe\frac{MV}{NI_1} \Rightarrow \frac{1}{q} = \frac{NI_1}{RoeMV} \Rightarrow Roe = q\frac{NI_1}{MV}$$

These can be implemented in the equation:

$$r_e = \frac{Roe(1-c)}{q} + cRoe = \frac{Roe(1-c)}{Roe\frac{MV}{NI_1}} + cq\frac{NI_1}{MV} = Roe(1-c)\frac{NI_1}{RoeMV} + cq\frac{NI_1}{MV}$$

$$= (1-c)\frac{NI_1}{MV} + cq\frac{NI_1}{MV} = (1 - c + cq)\frac{NI_1}{MV}$$

In this equation the discount rate for the shareholders is a function of reinvestment rate and Tobin's q which would be more preferable according to Ben-Horim and Callen as the "conventional growth rate g". is avoided. But if the firm has debts in its capital structure, the equation becomes a little bit different:

$$q = \frac{MV + D}{\frac{NI_1}{Roe} + D} = \frac{RoeD + RoeMV}{NI_1 + RoeD} \Rightarrow q(NI_1 + RoeD) = RoeD + RoeMV$$

$$= qNI_1 + qRoeD$$

$$= RoeD + RoeMV \Rightarrow qNI_1 = RoeD + RoeMV - qRoeD = (D + MV - qD)Roe$$

$$\Rightarrow Roe = \frac{qNI_1}{D + MV - qD} = \frac{qNI_1}{MV + (1 - q)D}$$

Substituting this into $MV = \frac{(1-c)NI_1}{r_e - cRoe}$ and solving for r_e yields:

$$MV = \frac{(1 - c)NI_1}{r_e - cRoe} = r_e - cRoe = \frac{(1 - c)NI_1}{MV} = r_e - \frac{cqNI_1}{MV + (1 - q)D} = \frac{(1 - c)NI_1}{MV}$$

$$\Rightarrow r_e = \frac{(1 - c)NI_1}{MV} + \frac{cqNI_1}{MV + (1 - q)D} = \left(1 - c + \frac{cqMV}{MV + (1 - q)D}\right)\frac{NI_1}{MV}$$

As Tobin's q, along with c, incorporates growth, the growth itself can be estimated through the equation above. From previous work, it is known that the discount rate can be expressed as the *dividend yield* $+ g$:

$$r_e = \frac{(1 - c)NI_1}{MV} + \frac{cqNI_1}{MV + (1 - q)D} = dividend\ yield + g$$

This can be used to estimate the g.

Ben-Horim and Callen concluded that, based on a sample of 98 firms from a time period of 1966-1985, the usage of Tobin's q in the discount rate had a more realistic look than traditional measures, as it impossible to say whether it is the "correct". It has been empirically shown that Tobin's q and the discount rate for shareholders have had an inversely relation. Because, Tobin's q grows as the company becomes more greater, almost as a monopoly, where the argument is that monopolies are able to capture the growth opportunities compared to competitive firms.

3.9.4 Normal distributed data

When the discount rates are computed, it is assumed that the data we use, returns and etc, are normal distributed. The probability distribution for stocks measures the probability that the actual return would be different from the expected. The problem appears when the data is not normal distributed. This can be due to skewness or (and) kurtosis. Skewness measures how asymmetrical the distribution is. If the distribution is positive skewed, then there is higher probability of large positive returns rather than large negative returns in the data and vice versa. The kurtosis measures the tails around the distribution. When the kurtosis is greater than 3, it implies that there is a high probability of extreme large and small returns. When the skewness is equal to 0, and a kurtosis to 3, then normal distribution exists. If this is not the case, one could possibly log the prices and computed the differences between the observations as:

$$\frac{\Delta P}{P} = \log\left(\frac{P_1}{P_0}\right) = \log(P_1) - \log(P_0)$$

There are other alternatives as increasing the number of observations, but this implies a trade-off since increasing the number of observations would mean a further step back in the company's history where its situation as environment, operations, competitions and etc could had been different.

While there are programs as excel, R, python and etc that could be used to compute the skewness and kurtosis, the formulas to test them manually are provided below:

$$Skewness = \frac{n}{(n-1)(n-2)}\sum \frac{(x_i - \bar{x})^3}{s^3}$$

$$Kurtosis = \left[\frac{n(n+1)}{(n-1)(n-2)(n-3)}\sum \frac{(x_i - \bar{x})^4}{s^4}\right] - \frac{3(n-1)^2}{(n-2)(n-3)}$$

Where n is the number of observations and s is the standard deviation:

$$s = \sqrt{\frac{1}{n-1} \sum_{i=1}^{n} (x_i - \bar{x})^2}$$

And $\bar{x}$ denotes the average of the observations:

$$\bar{x} = \frac{1}{n} \sum_{i=1}^{n} x_i$$

One common method to test whether the data is normal distributed is Jarque–Bera test, where its t statistic is computed as:

$$JB = \frac{n - m + 1}{6} \left(skew^2 + \frac{1}{4} (kurt - 3)^2 \right)$$

Where m is the number of estimated parameters. The null hypothesis of JB is that the t statistic is 0, implying that the data is normal disturbed as $skew = 0$ and $kurt = 3$.

While it seems complicated, it is not. An understanding of this provides one with the knowledge whether the risk associated with the discount rate is "well" represented. An example by using R. It is wondered whether the returns by Investor (Swedish investment company) from 2019-01 to 2020-01 could be considered as being normal distributed. Before computing the test, it is needed to retrieve the prices for Investor under this period. Start by downloading the following packages: PerformanceAnalytics, tseries, quantmod and timeSeries through library(). Thereafter, compute the ticker for Investor, which is "INVE-A.ST" on Yahoo Finance. All the values contained in Investor are cleared to avoid any interference by Investor <- NULL. Thereafter, retrieve the monthly data set through Yahoo Finance, where the price adjusted for splits and dividends ([,6]) is of interested and compute the returns (a <- na.omit(Return.calculate(Investor))). The steps are showed here:

```
library(PerformanceAnalytics)
library(tseries)
library(quantmod)
library(timeSeries)
```

```
ticker <- c("INVE-A.ST")
Investor <- NULL
for(ticker in tickers)
 Investor <- cbind(Investor, getSymbols(ticker, src="yahoo", from="2019-
01-01",
                        to  =  "2020-01-01",  periodicity="monthly",
auto.assign=FALSE) [,6])
a <- na.omit(Return.calculate(Investor))
jarque.bera.test(a)
```

The result is:

Jarque Bera Test

Data: a		
X-squared = 3.018	df = 2	p-value = 0.2211

The p value should be interpreted as the probability of us making a mistake if the null hypothesis is rejected. In statics, a significance level is used, denoted as α, to compare whether the null hypothesis can be rejected. The p value needs to be less than a for the null hypothesis to be rejected. For a significant level of 5%, the null hypothesis cannot be rejected which implies that the data returns from 2019-02 (one month disappears when we compute the returns) to 2020-01 can be considered to be normal distributed.

Chapter 4. Decision making

"Investment decision should be made on the basis of the most probable compounding of after-tax net worth with minimum risk."

-      *Warren Buffet*

"A wise man makes his own decisions. An ignorant man follows public opinion."

-      *Chinese Proverb*

While the quantifying of a stock price and its different components have been presented and discussed, it is important to understand whether the stock is attractive enough to be bought. The following section will wrap previous chapters and provide different tools as NPV, IRR and payback to comprehend how choices can be made. Further, as one progresses through the chapter, it is crucial that these tools need to be modified (and chosen) towards one preferences and circumstances.

4.0 Net Present Value

The *Net Present Value* (NPV) is the difference between the discounted cash inflows and outflows, implying in this context, the difference between the theorical price (discounted cash flows) and the actual stock price. NPV states the only acceptance, the buying of a stock, is if $NPV > 0$:

$$-P_{actual} + \sum_{t=1}^{n} \frac{CF_t}{(1+r)^t} + \frac{P_n}{(1+r)^n} > 0$$

Being logical as buying an overvalued stock would not make any sense. However, it cannot be assured that the theorical price, $\sum_{t=1}^{n} \frac{Div_t}{(1+r)^t} + \frac{P_n}{(1+r)^n}$, is accurate. Therefore, a margin of safety should be incorporated. The advantage of NPV is that it uses the concept time value of money. This could also be a disadvantage as, in some scenarios, it could be difficult to estimate the discount rate.

Another disadvantage of NPV is the mistake to disregard a stock with a higher potential as NPV does not take relativity into consideration. For instance, Stock A has a stock price of 5 SEK and a theorical of 10 SEK and Stock B has a stock price of 57 SEK and a theorical of 87 SEK. While Stock B has a higher NPV than A but a lesser expected return. This could be solved by relating the NPV to the actual price:

$$\frac{NPV}{P_{actual}} = \frac{-P_{actual} + \sum_{t=1}^{n} \frac{Div_t}{(1+r)^t} + \frac{P_n}{(1+r)^n}}{P_{actual}} = \frac{P_{theoretical} - P_{actual}}{P_{actual}}$$

This makes it easier to incorporate the margin of safety which can range from 10% to 200% (or more) conditioned on preferences.

Assume two dividend stocks, A and B, where their stock price are 25 SEK and 85 SEK. Following information are known:

P_0 for A	2019 (0)	2020 (1)	2021 (2)	2022 (3)
Div_t		2	2.08	2.12
r_e		0.1	0.1	0.07
g			0.04	0.02
$\displaystyle\sum_{t=1}^{T}\frac{Div_t}{(1+r_e)^t}$		1.82	1.72	
$\displaystyle\frac{\frac{Div_{T+1}}{r_{e T+1}}}{(1+r_e)^T}$			35.07	
P_0	38.60			
$\dfrac{NPV}{P}$	0.54			

P_0 for B	2019 (0)	2020 (1)	2021 (2)	2022 (3)
Div_t		5.00	5.25	5.36
r_e		0.09	0.09	0.06
g			0.05	0.02
$\displaystyle\sum_{t=1}^{T}\frac{Div_t}{(1+r_e)^t}$		4.59	4.42	
$\displaystyle\frac{\frac{Div_{T+1}}{r_{e T+1}}}{(1+r_e)^T}$			112.68	
P_0	121.69			
$\dfrac{NPV}{P}$	0.43			

Plugging these into the formulas, for A:

$$P_0 = \sum_{t=1}^{n}\frac{Div_1(1+g)^{t-1}}{(1+r_e)^t} + \frac{P_n}{(1+r_e)^n} = \sum_{t=1}^{2}\frac{Div_1(1+g)^{t-1}}{(1+r_e)^t} + \frac{\frac{Div_{n+1}}{r_{e n+1}} - g}{(1+r_e)^n}$$

$$= \frac{2}{(1+0.1)} + \frac{2(1+0.04)}{(1+0.1)^2} + \frac{1}{(1+0.1)^2}\frac{2(1+0.04)(1+0.02)}{0.07-0.02}$$

$$= 38.60$$

And for the NPV:

$$\frac{NPV_A}{P} = \frac{38.60 - 25}{25} = 0.54$$

For B:

$$P_0 = \sum_{t=1}^{n} \frac{Div_1(1+g)^{t-1}}{(1+r_e)^t} + \frac{P_n}{(1+r_e)^n} = \sum_{t=1}^{2} \frac{Div_1(1+g)^{t-1}}{(1+r_e)^t} + \frac{\frac{Div_{n+1}}{r_{e_{n+1}} - g}}{(1+r_e)^n}$$

$$= \frac{5}{(1+0.9)} + \frac{5(1+0.05)}{(1+0.9)^2} + \frac{1}{(1+0.9)^2} \frac{5(1+0.05)(1+0.02)}{0.06 - 0.02}$$

$$= 121.69$$

And for the NPV:

$$\frac{NPV_B}{P} = \frac{121.69 - 85}{85} = 0.43$$

Since $\frac{NPV_A}{P} > \frac{NPV_B}{P}$, stock A is more preferred. However, stock B should not be excluded if it could offer diversification benefits. Recall that the standard deviation of two stocks is written as:

$$\sigma_p^2 = w_A^2 \sigma_A^2 + 2w_A w_B \sigma_{A,B} + w_B^2 \sigma_B^2 \Rightarrow \sigma_p = \sqrt{w_A^2 \sigma_A^2 + 2w_A w_B \sigma_{A,B} + w_B^2 \sigma_B^2}$$

Where:

$$\sigma_{A,B} = \sigma_A \sigma_B \rho_{A,B}$$

$\rho_{A,B}$ is defined as the correlation between stock A and B. If the correlation was not perfectly positive than including both stocks in the portfolio will decrease the σ_p, ceteris paribus. It does not mean that the return is reduced of the portfolio as it is still possible to reduce the volatility of a portfolio while maintaining the return. But as it is out of scope how to optimise a portfolio, I would recommend books as "Modern Portfolio Theory and Investment Analysis" by Edwin J. Elton.

4.1 Internal Rate of Return

The *Internal Rate of Return* (IRR) is the discount rate that equalise the present value of cash flows with the actual stock price. With other words, it is the discount rate that equalise the theoretical stock price with the actual stock price:

$$-P_{actual} + \sum_{t=1}^{n} \frac{Div_t}{(1+r)^t} + \frac{P_n}{(1+r)^n} = 0 \Rightarrow \sum_{t=1}^{n} \frac{Div_t}{(1+r)^t} + \frac{P_n}{(1+r)^n} = P_{actual}$$

IRR states that a stock should be bought if IRR is greater than the estimated discount rate. Because, if the denominator is greater than de facto (IRR $> r_p$), the quotient would had been less, ceteris paribus. Therefore, the theorical price will be greater than the actual price given that IRR $> r_p$, suggesting a buy signal. IRR is frequently mentioned as the yield to maturity in bond market severing same function. In some cases, IRR could be as high as 80% which indicates that the dividends (if these are the cash flows) can be reinvested with an expected return of 80%, which is rare. Therefore, one should be careful of the interpretation by IRR because if the market valued a stock with a high discount rate, it could entail that something significantly negative will occur or has already happen but the book values has not been amended yet. Further, while stock A could have a higher IRR than B, it doesn't necessary mean that stock A should be invested in and not B because their NPV could be different conditioned on their estimated discount rate.

Let us the same example as for the NPV, but say that at the end of year 2, the stock is expected to be sold, hence the terminal value is:

$$\frac{Div_3}{r_{e_3} - g}$$

As before but where the two discount rates before the terminal value are unknown:

P_0 for A	2019 (0)	2020 (1)	2021 (2)	2022 (3)
Div_t		2	2.08	2.12
P_n			42.43	
r_e		?	?	0.07
IRR		0.37	0.37	
g			0.04	0.02
$\sum_{t=1}^{T} \dfrac{Div_t}{(1+r_e)^t}$		1.45	1.10	
$\dfrac{P_n}{(1+r_e)^T}$			22.45	
P_0	25			
P_0 for B	2019 (0)	2020 (1)	2021 (2)	2022 (3)
Div_t		5.00	5.25	5.36
P_n			107.10	
r_e		?	?	0.07
IRR		0.18	0.18	
g			0.05	0.02
$\sum_{t=1}^{T} \dfrac{Div_t}{(1+r_e)^t}$		4.24	3.77	
$\dfrac{P_n}{(1+r_e)^T}$			76.99	
P_0	85.00			

Putting it into the formulas, for A:

$$25 = \sum_{t=1}^{n} \frac{Div_t}{(1+IRR)^t} + \frac{P_n}{(1+r_e)^n} = \sum_{t=1}^{2} \frac{Div_1(1+g)^{t-1}}{(1+IRR)^t} + \frac{\frac{Div_{n+1}}{r_{e_{n+1}}-g}}{(1+IRR)^n}$$

$$= \frac{2}{(1+IRR)} + \frac{2(1+0.04)}{(1+IRR)^2} + \frac{42.43}{(1+IRR)^2}$$

By using problem solver in excel, $IRR = 0.37$.

For B:

$$85 = \sum_{t=1}^{n} \frac{Div_t}{(1+IRR)^t} + \frac{P_n}{(1+r_e)^n} = \sum_{t=1}^{2} \frac{Div_1(1+g)^{t-1}}{(1+IRR)^t} + \frac{\frac{Div_{+1}}{r_{en+1}-g}}{(1+IRR)^n}$$

$$= \frac{5}{(1+IRR)} + \frac{5(1+0.05)}{(1+IRR)^2} + \frac{107.10}{(1+IRR)^2}$$

Using problem solver in excel, $IRR = 0.18$.

If a more simplified model was assumed, then a problem solver is not needed. As with comparable discount, rewriting a growing (or non-growing) perpetuity model only requires some simple algebra:

$$P_0 = \frac{Div_1}{r_e - g} \Rightarrow P_0(r_e - g) = Div_1 \Rightarrow r_e = \frac{Div_1}{P_0} + g$$

As $\frac{Div_1}{P_0}$ is the dividend yield, the discount rate could be expressed, in this case, as the dividend yield plus the growth in dividends. This model could be used to derive an important concept that growth stocks carry a greater risk than value stocks which is discussed in the appendix.

4.2 Payback method

The *Payback method* (PM) is the time required before you receive back the investment cost. For instance, assume that a company is expected to distribute dividends of 15 SEK per share and the stock price is 113 SEK. Then the payback method would imply that it would take approximately 7.5 years before receiving back the amount invested:

$$\frac{113}{15} \approx 7.5 \; years \Rightarrow \frac{Investment\; cost}{cash\; flows} = Payback\; time$$

If you divide this quotient with 1:

$$\frac{1}{\frac{P_{actual}}{Div}} = \frac{Div}{P_{actual}} = dividend\; yield$$

So, assume that a stock has a dividend yield of 7% which is expected to remain constant, then the payback time would be:

$$\frac{1}{dividend\ yield} = \frac{1}{0.07} = 14.29\ years$$

As with comparable valuation, the ratios could tell the payback time. For instance, consider a P/E of 3.4, this would yield a payback time of 3.4 years:

$$\frac{P}{E} = \frac{Investment\ cost}{Net\ income} = 3.4\ years$$

The same goes for all the other ratios, including the actual stock price as the nominator, as with P/B, P/FCFF etc. The problem that could occur is that, going back to dividends, that the firm decides to distribute dividends of different seizes over the years. This could be amended by changing the denominator:

$$\frac{\{x|Investment\ cost - \sum_i^n Div_i, x > 0\}}{Div_{n+1}} + n = years$$

Which tells that each dividend per share from the stock price are subtract until it cannot be further subtracted (when it reaches 0) because the nominator would be negative in that case. When that point is reached, divide the dividend per share after the last one in the nominator. Each dividend subtracted in the nominator is equal to one year, hence the expression "$+n$". Assume a stock with the following expected dividends [1,3,4,2,5,6] for the coming years where the stock price today is 40 SEK. What is the payoff time?

$$\frac{\{x|Investment\ cost - \sum_i^n Div_i, x > 0\}}{Div_{n+1}} + n = \frac{40 - 1 - 3 - 4 - 2 - 5}{6} + 5$$
$$= 9.17\ years$$

One problem with the payback method is that it does not consider the present value of these cash flows. However, one could discount the dividends, net income, etc to amend for this.

4.3 Summary

The three tools (NPV, IRR and PM) are used differently conditioned on the context. One should be cautioned to use them simultaneously as they probably will yield different outcomes. Therefore, pros and cons should be thought of as they are being used.

Questions for chapter 4

1. The actual price for stock A is 40 SEK with dividends of 4 SEK per share. What is the NPV of stock A if the discount rate is 5%, growth 1% and the firm is assumed to be in a stable condition?

2. Stock B and C yields NPV of 200 and 130 SEK. Which one should be invested in if the stock price for B and C are 130 and 95 SEK?

3. It is unsure what theoretical price was retrieved from one of the analysts, where the NPV in relative to the actual price was calculated to be 30%. With stock price of 15 SEK, obtain the theorical price calculated by the analyst.

4. What is the implied discount rate for stock D with an expected consistent dividend of 3 SEK per share in year 3, growth of 2% and an actual stock price of 12.25 SEK?

5. Stock E announces it will distribute dividends of 5 SEK per share perpetually. With a stock price of 50 SEK, how long is the payback time?

6. An analyst said that the payback time of stock F is 11 years based on its consistent distribution of dividends. What is the implied dividend yield?

4.4 Appendix

The growing perpetuity model could be used to describe growth stocks as of greater risk by using the duration measure. It is more common to talk about the duration in fixed income securities than stocks as the duration (D) is a sensitivity measure for the price of a security to a change in the variable of interest (commonly the interest rate $- r$):

$$-\frac{1}{P}\frac{\partial P}{\partial r} = D$$

Where ∂ can be approximated to Δ:

$$-\frac{1}{P}\frac{\partial P}{\partial r} = D \Rightarrow \frac{\Delta P}{P} = -D * \Delta r$$

But for stocks, the duration can be defined as a sensitivity measure for the price of a stock to a change in the discount rate:

$$-\frac{1}{P}\frac{\partial P}{\partial r_e} = D \Rightarrow \frac{\Delta P}{P} = -D * \Delta r_e$$

The greater the D, the greater will the impact be on $\frac{\Delta P}{P}$ when the discount rate changes. Returning back to the growing perpetuity model:

$$P_0 = \frac{Div_1}{r_e - g} \Rightarrow -\frac{1}{P}\frac{\partial P}{\partial r_e} = -\frac{Div_1}{P}(-1)\frac{1}{(r_e - g)^2} = \frac{Div_1}{P}\frac{1}{(r_e - g)^2}$$

Where it is known that:

$$r_e = \frac{Div_1}{P_0} + g \Rightarrow \frac{Div_1}{P_0} = r_e - g$$

So:

$$-\frac{1}{P}\frac{\partial P}{\partial r_e} = \frac{Div_1}{P}\frac{1}{(r_e - g)^2} = (r_e - g)\frac{1}{(r_e - g)^2} = \frac{1}{r_e - g} = \frac{1}{\frac{Div_1}{P}} \Rightarrow \frac{\Delta P}{P}$$

$$= -\frac{1}{dividend\ yield}\Delta r_e$$

This describes that the lower the dividend yield is, the greater will the impact of a change in the discount rate be. As high growth stocks reinvest a lot of their earnings, their dividend yield is meager, stating that if the discount rate would decrease, its $\frac{\Delta P}{P}$ would increase in a greater scale than a more stable, low growth, stock. For instance, assume that stock A has a dividend yield of 3% and there is decrease of the discount rate by 1%, what is the expected price change:

$$\frac{\Delta P}{P} = -\frac{1}{dividend\ yield}\Delta r_e = -\frac{1}{0.03} * (-0.01) = 0.33 = 33\%$$

While it is understandable that high growth stocks, small cap, would normally be needed of a two-stage model (where we take the derivative of the discount rate), the conclusion will be the same regarding their risk.

It is interesting if we assume a non-growing perpetuity model and calculate $\Delta P/P$, then we could get an estimate what the new discount rate should be as $\Delta P/P$ changes:

$$P_0 = \frac{Div_1}{r_e - g} \Rightarrow -\frac{1}{P}\frac{\partial P}{\partial r_e} = -\frac{Div_1}{P}(-1)\frac{1}{r_e^2} = \frac{Div_1}{P}\frac{1}{r_e^2} \Rightarrow \frac{\Delta P}{P} = -\frac{1}{r_e}\Delta r_e = -\frac{r_{e_1} - r_{e_0}}{r_{e_0}}$$

$$= -\frac{r_{e_1}}{r_{e_0}} - 1 \Rightarrow r_{e_1} = \left(1 - \frac{\Delta P}{P}\right)r_{e_0}$$

This helps to see that if the return of a stock increases, then it must be because of the discount rate decreasing, or in other words, the required return of the investors decreasing, ceteris paribus. While this being a straightforward method to illustrate how the stock return is correlated with the discount rate, there are other variables to regard. It has been argued through research that stocks with higher dividend yield would have a lesser volatility.

Returning back to Ben-Horim and Callen (1989) work, with the help of Tobin's q, they could estimate the duration. They used the DDM to estimate the value of the equity

$$P_0 = \frac{Div_0(1 + g)}{r_e - g}$$

As Div_0 is considered to be a constant

$$-\frac{1}{P}\frac{\partial P}{\partial r} = \frac{\sum_{t=1}^{\infty}\frac{Div_0(1+g)^t}{(1+r_e)^t}t}{\frac{Div_0(1+g)}{r_e-g}} = \frac{r_e-g}{(1+g)}\sum_{t=1}^{\infty}\left(\frac{1+g}{1+r_e}\right)^t t$$

Denote $\frac{1+g}{1+r_e} = x$ so:

$$\frac{r_e-g}{(1+g)}\sum_{t=1}^{\infty}\left(\frac{1+g}{1+r_e}\right)^t t = \frac{r_e-g}{(1+g)}\sum_{t=1}^{\infty}x^t t$$

Further define $S(x) = \sum_{t=1}^{\infty}x^t$ so $S(x) = \frac{1}{(1-x)}$:

$$\frac{dS}{dx} = \sum_{t=1}^{\infty}x^{t-1}t = \frac{1}{(1-x)^2}$$

As $x = \frac{1+g}{1+r_e}$:

$$-\frac{1}{P}\frac{\partial P}{\partial r} = \frac{r_e-g}{(1+g)}\frac{dS}{dx} = \frac{r_e-g}{(1+g)}\frac{x}{(1-x)^2} = \frac{1+r_e}{r_e-g}$$

And since $g = cRoe$:

$$\frac{1+r_e}{r_e-g} = \frac{1+r_e}{r_e-cRoe}$$

From here, Ben-Horim and Callen uses earlier equation $MV = \frac{(1-c)NI_1}{r_e-cRoe}$ to substitute into the above to eliminate $r_e - cRoe$:

$$MV = \frac{(1-c)NI_1}{r_e-cRoe} \Rightarrow r_e - cRoe = \frac{(1-c)NI_1}{MV}$$

Hence:

$$\frac{1+r_e}{r_e-cRoe} = \frac{(1+r_e)MV}{(1-c)NI_1}$$

There were two equations from the subchapter about Tobin's q, the equation regarding a full equity firm:

$$r_e = (1 - c + cq)\frac{NI_1}{MV}$$

And non-full:

$$r_e = \left(1 - c + \frac{cqMV}{MV + (1 - q)D}\right)\frac{NI_1}{MV}$$

Hence the duration for an equity firm:

$$\frac{(1 + r_e)MV}{(1 - c)NI_1} = \frac{\left(1 + (1 - c + cq)\frac{NI_1}{MV}\right)MV}{(1 - c)NI_1} = \frac{MV + (1 - c + cq)NI_1}{(1 - c)NI_1}$$

$$= \frac{1}{1 - c}\left(\frac{NI_1}{MV} + 1 - c + cq\right)$$

And for a non-full equity firm:

$$\frac{(1 + r_e)MV}{(1 - c)NI_1} = \frac{\left[1 + \left(1 - c + \frac{cqMV}{MV + (1 - q)D}\right)\frac{NI_1}{MV}\right]MV}{(1 - c)NI_1}$$

$$= \frac{1}{1 - c}\left(\frac{NI_1}{MV} + 1 - c + \frac{cqMV}{MV + (1 - q)D}\right)$$

It can be seen that if $D = 0$, the equation of duration for equity and non would be identical

Baskin (1989)[56] examined the relationship between the dividend yield and risk, measured by the standard deviation of the returns. Baskin studied 2344 U.S. firms from 1967 to 1986. Before running the regression, Baskin used control variables as earning volatility, firms' size, debt and growth. The results suggested that there was a statistical negative relationship between the dividend yield and the volatility. Also, the payout showed to have a statistical relationship with the volatility. Interestingly, Allen & Rachim (1996) [57] received different results where they made a similar regression by focusing on 173 Australian listed companies from 1972 to 1985. Because Allen & Rachim

---

[56] Baskin, J. (1989). Dividend policy and the volatility of common stock. Journal of Portfolio Management, 15, 19-25

[57] Allen, D.E. & Rachim, V.S. (1996). Dividend policy and stock price volatility: Australian evidence. Applied Financial Economics, 6(2), 175-188.

suspected multicollinearity by only including the dividend yield and payout, they included control variables as earning volatility, log of firms' size, long term debt and growth in assets. Allen & Rachim displayed different regressions to give perspectives on how the dividend yield and payout acted. In all of these regressions, the dividend yield showed no statistical significance while the payout showed a statistical negative relationship. Baskin actually dropped the payout variable as he suspected multicollinearity, but he did not run different regressions to see whether it was the payout or dividend yield that was significant.

Despite Baskin and Allen & Rachim results, there is still a debate on how dividends affect the volatility, as there are conflicting results. Hussainey, Mgbame & Chijoke-Mgbame (2011)[58] applied the same regression towards companies in the UK from 1998 to 2007. They did not display the number of companies they had in their sample, but they retrieved a total sum of 123 of observations. In most of their regressions, dividend yield and the payout had a negative statistical relationship with the volatility. Hashemijoo, Ardekani & Younesi (2012)[59] reached the same conclusion while applying the regressions towards Malaysian stock market where a sample of 84 companies from the 142 consumer product companies where used from 2005 to 2010. As for Hussainey, Mgbame & Chijoke-Mgbame, the regressions by Hashemijoo, Ardekani & Younesi changed in their significance regarding the dividend yield and payout when someone of them were left out. The same conclusion could be draw by Ahmad, Alrjoub & Alrabba (2018)[60] results where they were interested of the Amman Stock exchange from a period of 2010 to 2016 with a sample of 228 forms. Concluding, it is hard to decide whether the dividend yield or the payout

---

[58] Hussainey, K., Mgbame, C.O., & Chijoke-Mgbame, A.M. (2011). Dividend policy and share price volatility: UK evidence.. The Journal of Risk Finance. 12. 10.1108/15265941111100076.

[59] Hashemijoo, M., Ardekani, A. & Younesi, N. (2012). The Impact of Dividend Policy on Share Price Volatility in The Malaysian Stock Market. Journal of Business Studies Quaterly. 4. 111-129.

[60] Ahmad, M.A., Alrjoub, A.M., & Alrabba, H.M. (2018). The Effect of Dividend Policy on Stock Price Volatility: Empirical Evidence from Amman Stock Exchange. *Academy of Accounting and Financial Studies Journal, 22.*

is the main determinant of this negative relationship as they are intimate. But, the majority of research suggests that both dividend yield and payout act as a negative force against the volatility.

Leibowitz, Sorensen & Nicholas (1989)[61] stated that DDM duration is *"overly simplistic because it lacks the dynamic elements of cause and effect"*. Since, it assumes that changes in the discount rate are unrelated to the future growth of dividends. However, in practice a change in inflation could cause the growth rate to change but also the discount rate indirectly as changes in inflation might cause a change in interest rate and capital market rates in generic. Leibowitz, Sorensen & Nicholas consider the compounded interest rate to be a better measure, so instead of $-\partial P/\partial r_e$ it would be:

$$-\frac{\partial lnP}{\partial r_e}$$

Where:

$$P = \frac{Div_0(1+g)}{r_e - g}$$

So:

$$-\frac{\partial lnP}{\partial r_e} = -\frac{1}{r_e - g}$$

But as the growth rate is consider of importance, total differentiation would be used:

$$\frac{dP}{P} = dlnP = \frac{\partial lnP}{\partial r_e}dr_e + \frac{\partial lnP}{\partial g}dg$$

Leibowitz, Sorensen & Nicholas defined r_e to be a function of the nominal interest rate (i) and a function of the equity market risk premium ($h[I, r, ...]$)and the growth rate as a constant growth parameter (g_0) plus growth rate sensitivity

---

[61] Leibowitz, M., Sorensen, E., Robert D. Arnott, & H. Nicholas Hanson. (1989). A Total Differential Approach to Equity Duration. Financial Analysts Journal, 45(5), 30-37. Retrieved May 31, 2020, from www.jstor.org/stable/4479256

to real interest rate (y) multiplied by real interest rate (r) and inflation flow through parameter (λ) multiplied by an inflation component (I). So

$$\frac{\partial lnP}{\partial r_e}dr_e + \frac{\partial lnP}{\partial g}dg = -\frac{1}{r_e - g}(dk - dg)$$

where

$$dk = dr + dI + \frac{\partial h}{\partial I}dI + \frac{\partial h}{\partial r}dr$$

And

$$dg = ydr + \lambda dI$$

Hence

$$\frac{dP}{P} = -\frac{1}{r_e - g}\left(1 - y + \frac{\partial h}{\partial r}\right)dr - \frac{1}{r_e - g}\left(1 - \lambda + \frac{\partial h}{\partial I}\right)dI$$

Leibowitz, Sorensen & Nicholas made the separation that $-\frac{1}{r_e-g}\left(1 - y + \frac{\partial h}{\partial r}\right)$ represented the sensitivity to changes in real rate of interest and $-\frac{1}{r_e-g}\left(1 - \lambda + \frac{\partial h}{\partial I}\right)$ as sensitivity to changes in the inflation expectations. So, firms with high levels of inflation flow-through (λ approaching) may have low interest rate sensitivities while companies that adversely affected by an increase in real interest rate would have a focus on interest rate sensitivity. These calculations could give a better insight to the duration of the stock as it considers other effect than solely the discount rate.

Solution Manual

Solutions chapter 1

Question 1

$$P_0 \prod_{t=1}^{n}(1+r_t) = 80(1+0.05)^3(1+0.08)^2 = 108$$

Question 2

$$P_0 = \sum_{i=5}^{n} \frac{Div_i}{(1+r)^i} + \frac{P_{i+1}}{(1+r)^{i+1}} = \frac{6}{(1+0.1)^5} + \frac{130}{(1+0.1)^6} \approx 77.11$$

Question 3

$$P_0 = \sum_{i=1}^{n} \frac{Div_i}{(1+r)^i} + \frac{P_n}{(1+r)^n}$$

$$= \frac{6}{(1+0.07)} + \frac{6(1+0.01)}{(1+0.07)(1+0.06)}$$

$$+ \frac{6(1+0.01)^2}{(1+0.07)(1+0.06)(1+0.09)}$$

$$+ \frac{6(1+0.01)^3}{(1+0.07)(1+0.06)(1+0.09)(1+0.08)}$$

$$+ \frac{6(1+0.01)^4}{(1+0.07)(1+0.06)(1+0.09)(1+0.08)(1+0.1)}$$

$$+ \frac{240}{(1+0.07)(1+0.06)(1+0.09)(1+0.08)(1+0.1)} \approx 188.19$$

Question 4

$$P_0 = \sum_{i=1}^{n} \frac{Div_i}{(1+r)^i} + \frac{P_n}{(1+r)^n}$$

$$= \frac{Div_i}{(1+r_1)} + \frac{Div_2}{r_1}\left(1 - \frac{(1+g)^4}{(1+r_1)^4}\right)\frac{1}{(1+r_1)} + \frac{P_5}{(1+r)^5} \approx 193.40$$

$$P_0 = \sum_{i=1}^{n} \frac{Div_i}{(1+r)^i} + \frac{P_n}{(1+r)^n}$$

$$= \frac{Div_1}{(1+r_1)} + \frac{Div_1(1+g)}{r_1}\left(1 - \frac{(1+g)^4}{(1+r_1)^4}\right)\frac{1}{(1+r_1)}$$

$$+ \frac{\frac{Div_1(1+g)^5}{r_1 - g}}{(1+r_1)^5} \approx 97.22$$

The constant assumed discount rate with a known price yields the highest price as the accumulate static discount rates at year 1 are lesser then the dynamic. Further, the dividends are small in relative to the expected sell price, thereafter the unknown stock price model, growing perpetuity, estimated the smallest.

Question 5

$$P_0 = \frac{Div_i}{r_e}\frac{1}{(1+r_e)^{i-1}} = \frac{11.5}{0.06}\frac{1}{(1+0.06)^5} \approx 143.22$$

Question 6

$$P_0 = \sum_{i=1}^{n} \frac{Div_i}{(1+r)^i} + \frac{P_n}{(1+r)^n}$$

$$= \frac{Div_1}{(1+r)} + \frac{Div_2}{r-g}\left(1 - \left(\frac{1+g}{1+r}\right)^{n-1}\right)\frac{1}{(1+r)} + \frac{Div_{n+1}}{r-g}\frac{1}{(1+r)^n}$$

$$= \frac{4}{(1+0.14)} + \frac{4(1+0.07)}{0.14 - 0.07}\left(1 - \left(\frac{1+0.07}{1+0.14}\right)^4\right)\frac{1}{(1+0.14)}$$

$$+ \frac{4(1+0.07)^4(1+0.02)}{0.06 - 0.02}\frac{1}{(1+0.14)^5} \approx 84.96$$

Question 7

$$P_0 = \sum_{i=1}^{n} \frac{Div_i}{(1+r)^i} + \frac{P_n}{(1+r)^n}$$

$$= \frac{10}{(1+0.13)} + \frac{10(1+0.05)}{(1+0.13)^2} + \frac{10(1+0.05)^2}{(1+0.13)^3} + \frac{10(1+0.05)^3}{(1+0.13)^4}$$

$$+ \frac{10(1+0.05)^4}{(1+0.13)^5} + \frac{10(1+0.05)^4(1+0.045)}{(1+0.13)^5(1+0.11)}$$

$$+ \frac{10(1+0.05)^4(1+0.045)^2}{(1+0.13)^5(1+0.11)^2}$$

$$+ \frac{10(1+0.05)^4(1+0.045)^2(1+0.02)}{0.07-0.02} \cdot \frac{1}{(1+0.14)^5(1+0.11)^2}$$

$$\approx 169.75$$

Solutions chapter 2

Question 1

$$FCFE = Net\ income\ (1 - RR_n) - (Debt\ paid - Debt\ issued) = 10(1 - 0.7) + 5$$
$$= 8\ MSEK$$

Question 2

$$FCFF = CFOA + interest\ expenses\ (1 - tc) - CAPEX$$

$$FCFE = CFOA - CAPEX - (Debt\ paid - Debt\ issued)$$

$$FCFF = 100 + 6(1 - 0.2) - 20 = 84.8$$

$$FCFE = 100 - 20 - (50 - 35.4) = 65.4$$

$$P_{Stock\ A} = \frac{\frac{65.4}{4} * 1.01}{0.07 - 0.01} \approx 275.23$$

Question 3

$$P_0 = \frac{FCFE_{per\ share}(1+g)}{r_e - g} \Rightarrow FCFE_{per\ share} = \frac{P_0(r_e - g)}{1+g} = \frac{10(0.06 - 0.015)}{1 + 0.015}$$

$$\approx 0.44$$

Question 4

$$EV = \frac{FCFF(1+g)}{WACC - g} \Rightarrow FCFF = \frac{EV(WACC - g)}{1+g} = \frac{1000(0.08 - 0.02)}{1 + 0.02} \approx 58.82$$

To retrieve the FCFE from FCFF, both *interest expenses* $(1 - tc)$ and (*Debt paid* − *Debt issued*) have to be subtracted:

$$FCFE = FCFF - interest\ expenses\ (1 - tc) - (Debt\ paid - Debt\ issued)$$
$$= 58.82 - 9(1 - 0.35) - (20.5 - 10) \approx 42.47$$

$$P_0 = \frac{FCFE_{per\ share}(1+g)}{r_e - g} = \frac{\frac{42.47}{2}(1 + 0.02)}{0.1 - 0.02} \approx 279.75$$

Question 5

$$FCFE_1 = 100 - 20 - (50 - 35.4) = 65.4$$

$$FCFE_2 = 150 - 25 - (30 - 20) = 115$$

$$FCFE_3 = 120 - 23 - (25 - 25) = 97$$

$$P_0 = \frac{\frac{65.4}{2}}{(1 + 0.1)} + \frac{\frac{115}{2}}{(1 + 0.1)^2} + \frac{\frac{97}{2}}{0.08} \frac{1}{(1 + 0.1)^2} \approx 578.28$$

Question 6

$$RI_{1,per\ share} = \frac{600 - 0.09 * 5500}{15} = 7$$

$$RI_{2,per\ share} = \frac{625 - 0.09 * 6000}{15} \approx 5.67$$

$$RI_{2,per\ share} = \frac{800 - 0.06 * 6600}{15} \approx 26.93$$

$$P_0 = \frac{5500}{15} + \frac{7}{(1 + 0.09)} + \frac{5.67}{(1 + 0.09)^2} + \frac{26.93}{0.06} \frac{1}{(1 + 0.09)^2} \approx 755.64$$

Question 7

$$EV = \frac{FCFF_1}{WACC - g} = P_0 * outstanding\ shares + Debts - Cash \Rightarrow P_0$$

$$= \frac{\frac{FCFF_1}{WACC - g} + Cash - Debts}{outstanding\ shares} = \frac{\frac{120}{0.07 - 0.005} + 10 - 50}{4}$$

$$\approx 418.57$$

Question 8

$$P_1 = \frac{EV_0 + EV_0 \left(\frac{r_{wacc_0} - r_{wacc_1}}{r_{wacc_1}}\right) - D_1 + C_1}{S_0 - \frac{\Delta D}{P_0}}$$

$$= \frac{1000 + 1000 \left(\frac{0.07 - 0.05}{0.05}\right) - 500 + 30}{200 - \frac{200}{20}} \approx 4.89$$

Solutions chapter 3

Question 1

$$\frac{D}{E} \Rightarrow 1 + \frac{D}{E} = \frac{E + D}{E}$$

Divide this by 1:

$$\frac{1}{\frac{E+D}{E}} = \frac{E}{E+D} = \frac{E}{TA}$$

Where:

$$1 - \frac{E}{TA} = \frac{D}{TA}$$

So:

$$\frac{1}{1 + \frac{D}{E}} \approx 0.74$$

And

$$1 - \frac{E}{TA} = 1 - 0.74 = 0.26$$

Hence:

$$WACC = \frac{E}{TA} r_e + \frac{D}{TA} r_D (1 - t_c) = 0.74 * 0.07 + 0.26 * 0.03 * (1 - 0.3) \approx 0.057$$

Question 2

$$\frac{E}{D} \Rightarrow 1 + \frac{E}{D} = \frac{D+E}{D}$$

Divide this by 1:

$$\frac{1}{\frac{D+E}{D}} = \frac{D}{D+E} = \frac{D}{TA}$$

Where:

$$1 - \frac{D}{TA} = \frac{E}{TA}$$

So:

$$\frac{1}{1+\dfrac{E}{D}} \approx 0.69$$

And

$$1 - \frac{D}{TA} = 1 - 0.69 = 0.31$$

To get the levered beta to later calculate the cost of equity through CAPM:

$$\beta_L = \beta_u \left(1 + \frac{D}{E}(1 - t_c)\right)$$

Where:

$$\frac{1}{\dfrac{E}{D}} = \frac{D}{E} \approx 2.22$$

So:

$$\beta_L = 0.7\left(1 + 2.22(1 - 0.3)\right) \approx 1.79$$

As for CAPM:

$$r_e = r_f + \beta_L\left(r_{mkt} - r_f\right)$$

Where:

$$r_{mkt} = 0.1$$

And:

$$r_{mkt} - r_f = riskpremium = 0.08 \Rightarrow 0.1 - r_f = 0.08 \Rightarrow r_f = 0.1 - 0.08 = 0.02$$

So:

$$r_e = 0.02 + 1.79 * 0.08 \approx 0.16$$

Concluding that WACC is equal to:

$$WACC = \frac{E}{TA}r_e + \frac{D}{TA}r_D(1 - t_c) = 0.31 * 0.16 + 0.69 * 0.03 * (1 - 0.3) \approx 0.064$$

Question 3

$$\left(1 + \frac{(1-t_c)D_L}{E_L}\right)\frac{1}{n}\sum_t^n \beta_{U_t} = \beta_L = \left(1 + \frac{650}{1000}(1 - 0.3)\right)0.875 = 1.27$$

Hence, CAPM is equal to:

$$r_e = 0.04 + 1.27 * (0.11 - 0.04) \approx 0.129$$

Question 4

$$P_0 = \frac{Div_1}{r_e - g} \Rightarrow r_e = \frac{Div_1}{P_0} + g = \frac{2}{15} + 0.02 \approx 0.15$$

Question 5
Using

$$\frac{CF_t}{(1+r_d)^t} = \frac{CF_t * d_t}{(1+r_f)^t} \Rightarrow CF_t = \frac{CF_t * d_t}{(1+r_f)^t}(1+r_d)^t \Rightarrow \frac{CF_t(1+r_f)^t}{CF_t * d_t} = (1+r_d)^t$$

$$\Rightarrow \frac{1+r_f}{\sqrt[t]{d_t}} - 1 = r_d$$

And

$$\frac{\frac{CF_t}{i}}{\left(1+\frac{r_d}{i}\right)^{it}} = \frac{\frac{CF_t}{i} * d_t}{\left(1+\frac{r_f}{i}\right)^{it}} \Rightarrow \frac{\left(1+\frac{r_f}{i}\right)^{it}}{d_t} = \left(1+\frac{r_d}{i}\right)^{it} \Rightarrow r_d = \left(\frac{\left(1+\frac{r_f}{i}\right)}{\sqrt[it]{d_t}} - 1\right) * i$$

Annual:

$$r_d = \frac{1+r_f}{\sqrt[t]{d_t}} = \frac{1+0.03}{\sqrt[1]{0.78}} - 1 \approx 0.32$$

Quarterly:

$$r_d = \left(\frac{\left(1 + \frac{r_f}{i}\right)}{\sqrt[it]{d_t}} - 1 \right) * i = \left(\frac{\left(1 + \frac{0.03}{4}\right)}{\sqrt[4]{0.78}} - 1 \right) * 4 \approx 0.29$$

Monthly:

$$r_d = \left(\frac{\left(1 + \frac{r_f}{i}\right)}{\sqrt[it]{d_t}} - 1 \right) * i = \left(\frac{\left(1 + \frac{0.03}{12}\right)}{\sqrt[12]{0.78}} - 1 \right) * 12 \approx 0.28$$

Solutions chapter 4

Question 1

$$P_0 = \frac{Div_1}{r_e - g} = \frac{4(1 + 0.01)}{0.05 - 0.01} = 101$$

$$\frac{NPV}{P_a} = \frac{101 - 40}{40} = 1.525$$

Question 2

$$\frac{NPV}{P_a} _{for\ B} = \frac{200 - 130}{130} \approx 0.54$$

$$\frac{NPV}{P_a} _{for\ C} = \frac{130 - 95}{95} \approx 037$$

Stock C should be selected.

Question 3

$$\frac{NPV}{P_a} = \frac{P_0 - P_a}{P_a} \Rightarrow P_0 = \frac{NPV}{P_a} P_a + P_a = 0.3 * 15 + 15 = 19.5$$

Question 4

$$P_0 = \frac{Div_3}{r_e - g} \frac{1}{(1 + r_e)^2} = 12.25 = \frac{3}{r_e - 0.02} \frac{1}{(1 + r_e)^2}$$

Through excel problem solver, the $r_e \approx 0.19$.

Question 5

$$\frac{Cost}{Cash\ inflow} = \frac{50}{5} = 10\ years$$

Question 6

$$\frac{Cost}{Cash\ inflow} = payback\ time = \frac{1}{Div\ yield} \Rightarrow Div\ yield$$

$$= \frac{1}{payback\ time} = \frac{1}{11} = 0.09$$

www.ingramcontent.com/pod-product-compliance
Lightning Source LLC
Chambersburg PA
CBHW070551220526
45467CB00003B/1169